**IMMIGRATION IN THE 21ST CENTURY:
POLITICAL, SOCIAL AND ECONOMIC ISSUES**

CAREER OPTIMISM AND SELF-EFFICACY IN IMMIGRANTS

IMMIGRATION IN THE 21ST CENTURY: POLITICAL, SOCIAL AND ECONOMIC ISSUES

Additional books in this series can be found on Nova's website under the Series tab.

Additional e-books in this series can be found on Nova's website under the eBooks tab.

BUSINESS ISSUES, COMPETITION AND ENTREPRENEURSHIP

Additional books in this series can be found on Nova's website under the Series tab.

Additional e-books in this series can be found on Nova's website under the eBooks tab.

IMMIGRATION IN THE 21ST CENTURY:
POLITICAL, SOCIAL AND ECONOMIC ISSUES

CAREER OPTIMISM AND SELF-EFFICACY IN IMMIGRANTS

CHARLES P. CHEN
AND
TARA K. KENNEDY

Copyright © 2018 by Nova Science Publishers, Inc.

All rights reserved. No part of this book may be reproduced, stored in a retrieval system or transmitted in any form or by any means: electronic, electrostatic, magnetic, tape, mechanical photocopying, recording or otherwise without the written permission of the Publisher.

We have partnered with Copyright Clearance Center to make it easy for you to obtain permissions to reuse content from this publication. Simply navigate to this publication's page on Nova's website and locate the "Get Permission" button below the title description. This button is linked directly to the title's permission page on copyright.com. Alternatively, you can visit copyright.com and search by title, ISBN, or ISSN.

For further questions about using the service on copyright.com, please contact:
Copyright Clearance Center
Phone: +1-(978) 750-8400   Fax: +1-(978) 750-4470   E-mail: info@copyright.com.

NOTICE TO THE READER

The Publisher has taken reasonable care in the preparation of this book, but makes no expressed or implied warranty of any kind and assumes no responsibility for any errors or omissions. No liability is assumed for incidental or consequential damages in connection with or arising out of information contained in this book. The Publisher shall not be liable for any special, consequential, or exemplary damages resulting, in whole or in part, from the readers' use of, or reliance upon, this material. Any parts of this book based on government reports are so indicated and copyright is claimed for those parts to the extent applicable to compilations of such works.

Independent verification should be sought for any data, advice or recommendations contained in this book. In addition, no responsibility is assumed by the publisher for any injury and/or damage to persons or property arising from any methods, products, instructions, ideas or otherwise contained in this publication.

This publication is designed to provide accurate and authoritative information with regard to the subject matter covered herein. It is sold with the clear understanding that the Publisher is not engaged in rendering legal or any other professional services. If legal or any other expert assistance is required, the services of a competent person should be sought. FROM A DECLARATION OF PARTICIPANTS JOINTLY ADOPTED BY A COMMITTEE OF THE AMERICAN BAR ASSOCIATION AND A COMMITTEE OF PUBLISHERS.

Additional color graphics may be available in the e-book version of this book.

Library of Congress Cataloging-in-Publication Data

Names: Chen, Charles P., author. | Kennedy, Tara K., author.
Title: Career optimism and self-efficacy in immigrants / Authors, Charles P. Chen and Tara K. Kennedy.
Description: Hauppauge : Nova Science Publishers, Inc., [2017] | Series: Immigration in the 21st century: political, social and economic issues business issues, competition and entrepreneurship | Includes bibliographical references and index.
Identifiers: LCCN 2018008638 (print) | LCCN 2018013575 (ebook) | ISBN 9781536132434 (ebook) | ISBN 9781634854306 (softcover)
Subjects: LCSH: Immigrants--Canada. | Immigrants--Vocational guidance--Canada. | Immigrants--Employment--Canada. | Career development--Canada.
Classification: LCC JV7220 (ebook) | LCC JV7220 .C54 2018 (print) | DDC 331.702086/9120971--dc23
LC record available at https://lccn.loc.gov/2018008638

Published by Nova Science Publishers, Inc. † New York

CONTENTS

Acknowledgments		vii
About the Authors		ix
Chapter 1	Introduction	1
Chapter 2	Life-Careers of Immigrants	9
Chapter 3	Research Process	31
Chapter 4	Life-Career Themes	41
Chapter 5	Career Optimism and Self-Efficacy	75
References		93
Appendix: Interview Questions		105
Index		117

ACKNOWLEDGMENTS

The authors would like to acknowledge and thank the support from the Social Sciences and Humanities Research Council of Canada (SSHRC). The completion of this book project was supported in part by a research grant awarded to Professor Charles P. Chen from SSHRC. *Standard Grant Program. Award No. 410-2009-2394.*

ABOUT THE AUTHORS

Charles P. Chen, PhD, is Professor of Counselling and Clinical Psychology and a Canada Research Chair at the University of Toronto (UofT). He is a *Distinguished Honorary Professor* and *Guest Chair Professor* at more than 10 major universities around the world. He is a Fellow of the Canadian Psychological Association and a noted social scientist in Canadian Who's Who and Who's Who in the World. As well, he is an award-winning professor for Excellence in Graduate Teaching at UofT.

Charles is a keynote/plenary speaker and regular presenter at conferences, and has been a distinguished guest speaker in various academic and professional contexts around the world over 170 times. He is also a featured expert in news media. His works include 6 scholarly/research books, 12 book chapters, and over 50 refereed journal articles. His book "Career Endeavour (Ashgate, 2006)" received the best counselling book award in Canada. According to Google Scholar, professor Charles P. Chen is one of the Top 9 most cited authors in literature regarding postmodern constructivist and constructionist studies within the realm of vocational and career psychology.

Tara Kennedy, M.A., is a Psychologist based in Halifax, Nova Scotia, Canada. She obtained her M.A. in Clinical and Counselling Psychology at the University of Toronto. Tara provides psychological services to adolescents and adults who present with a variety of mental health concerns. Tara believes that individuals do not need a diagnosis to seek psychological help, but sees the therapeutic process as being able to increase one's well-being, joy, and commitment to their values. Tara has also received specialized training in conducting psycho-educational assessments, which help to identify cognitive functioning impairments and learning/attention-related difficulties.

The cornerstone of Tara's therapeutic practice includes Acceptance and Commitment Therapy (ACT). In short, this practice teaches psychological skills to explore and manage painful thoughts and feelings effectively, ultimately allowing for goal-oriented action. Tara also addresses the importance of self-responsibility, accountability, and empowerment within the therapeutic process, wherein the client is responsible for actively engaging and applying techniques from therapy to his/her life. Through the use of therapeutic tools, Tara works with her clients to identify emotional blocks and difficulties, ultimately allowing for personal growth and well-being. Therapeutic tools that Tara often draws upon include mindfulness training, guided imagery, relaxation, goal setting and positive challenges, lifestyle recommendations, and awareness of the mind-body connection.

Chapter 1

INTRODUCTION

OVERVIEW

This book presents a research study that examined the retraining and career development experiences of new and professional immigrants in Canada. The study intended to provide an in-depth perspective into the influence of immigrants' optimism and self-efficacy on their retraining and career development experiences. Using a qualitative methodology, in-depth interviews were conducted and a grounded theory approach was employed to analyze the data. Central themes within participant narratives emerged and key results were introduced. Participants' experiences included a myriad of barriers and challenges, yet many viewed this experience as a positive opportunity for growth and development. The results explored differences between optimists' and pessimists' retraining and career development experiences, as well as the role of self-efficacy within immigrants' career development. Results have implications for career and vocational psychology literature, practice, and career counselling, and include suggestions for future researchers.

BACKGROUND

Canada increasingly depends on immigration as a major strategy for nation building, development, and economic well-being. In fact, from July to September of 2010, 84,200 immigrants came to Canada, which makes it the highest number of immigrants to migrate to Canada in any quarter since 1971 (Statistics Canada, 2010). However, Canada's ability to integrate immigrants into its workforce has been inadequate, as many new and professional immigrants remain unemployed or underemployed (when one is over-qualified for their current job) for a significant period of time. For instance, while 80% of new immigrants find work within two years of immigrating, only 42% find work within their area of expertise (Canadian Labour and Business Centre, 2003). Accordingly, many new immigrants enroll in training programs soon after coming to Canada in an effort to qualify for work, relearn particular skills, gain knowledge, and further their education. In fact, in a recent study, 45% of new immigrants had already pursued some type of training just six months after arriving to Canada (Statistics Canada, 2003). Despite this representative statistic, as well as the significance that training programs provide in an immigrant's overall transition process, there is a paucity of research that investigates immigrant experience in training programs. Furthermore, the impact of individual characteristics on immigrants' experience in their training programs has yet to be explored.

Not only is the number of new immigrants arriving into Canada increasing, but recent immigrants in Canada are more educated than past immigrants, and are twice as likely as the Canadian born population to have a university degree (Statistics Canada, 2008). As such, the majority of immigrants are accepted into Canada under the Skilled Worker Program as a means of providing appropriate employment for new immigrants by filling employment shortages in the labour market (Citizenship and Immigration Canada, 2007). The Skilled Worker Program classifies skilled workers as individuals who are selected as permanent residents based on their ability to become economically established in Canada (Citizenship and Immigration Canada, 2007). The classification of a skilled worker is contingent upon the

Introduction 3

individual's education, knowledge and proficiency of English and/or French, additional work experience requirements, as well as other requirements that demonstrate the individual's ability to be economically established in Canada (Citizenship and Immigration Canada, 2007). Despite the intentions of the Skilled Worker Program, new and professional immigrants who enter Canada under this program face an extremely arduous process in search of a career in their trained field. In fact, ample literature (Chen, 2008; Dean & Wilson, 2009; Mak, Westwood, & Ishiyama, 1994; Reitz, 2001) suggests that the majority of immigrants experience various unforeseen consequences and hardships in terms of their career development. For instance, immigrants tend to be generally shocked after arriving into Canada when they are not able to secure a job or career within their area of expertise. This is largely due to the fact that before moving to Canada, they are given the impression that Canada has high economic well-being, is in demand of professional and educated immigrants, and provides a good opportunity for employment (Canada Updates, 2009). However, as much of the research suggests, immigrants face a myriad of barriers and stressors almost immediately after arriving into the country.

As a result of the difficult transition process and career-related hardships (particularly under/unemployment), many new immigrants experience many stress-related outcomes including anxiety, depression, worry, tension, irritation, and frustration (Dean & Wilson, 2009). Additionally, regardless of the fact that new immigrants may be highly educated, skilled, and may hold recognizable credentials, the majority of them will experience significant cross-cultural barriers (Mak, Westwood, & Ishiyama, 1994). Aside from the fact that the majority of new Canadian immigrants held some type of professional position in their host country (Kirkbride, Tang, & Ko, 1989), they experience distress and difficulties upon entering Canada with regard to securing a career within their area of expertise. Correspondingly, it is not surprising that a vast number of new immigrants transitioning into Canada are motivated to take some type of training course to further their knowledge, language skills, and education, as a means of managing their transition to Canada and corresponding career-related difficulties (Reitz, 2001; Statistics Canada, 2003). Despite the capacious number of immigrants who are or have been enrolled in a training program, there has been no research to date that has subjectively examined Canadian immigrants' experience in training or educational programs.

Research in this field has thus far explored the difficulties that new immigrants experience, such as under/unemployment, cross-cultural differences, and additional barriers associated with their career search and general transition to Canada (Dean & Wilson, 2009; Mak et al., 1994). Despite a recent interest in the investigation of immigrants' subjective understandings of this matter (Jafari, Baharlou & Mathias, 2010; Rastogi, 2007) research has not yet explored new and professional immigrants' subjective narratives surrounding their personal experience within their training program. Furthermore, despite the rich history and development of vocational psychology, current literature fails to consider the career development process of new immigrants. For example, existing literature (Career Development Assessment and Counseling; Perceived Occupational Opportunity Scale; Perceived Occupational Discrimination Scale) has been ameliorated to apply theory, assessment techniques, and new approaches to culturally diverse populations (Hartung, Vandiver, Leong, Pope, Niles, & Farrow, 1998; Herr, Cramer, & Niles, 2004; Super, 1990). However, current literature remains insufficient in providing an understanding of immigrants' career development process. Moreover, despite the inherent connection between the new immigrants' involvement in re-training and the impact of such learning experiences on these immigrants' vocational well-being, no empirical research exists that examines the subjective perceptions of immigrant experience during training or re-education programs. New knowledge in this terrain is yet to be built for vocational psychology. This study's objectives were to contribute to the body of knowledge surrounding new and professional immigrants' career development, vocational psychology, immigrant psychology, career counselling, and cross-cultural adjustment by exploring their subjective experience of their transition in Canada and corresponding career-related training program. Therefore, subsequent to gaining an in-depth exploration of immigrants' re-learning experience in training programs, this study aimed to propose a framework

Introduction 5

that provides insight into the underlying constructs of immigrants' career development experience.

Psychological well-being is a major determinant of one's experience within a given circumstance as well as its influence on one's psychological adjustment or transition period. Psychological well-being can include various influencing concepts; however, both optimism and self-efficacy are seen by the present researcher as key personal concepts that may influence one's transition and retraining experience. Self-efficacy is a concept coined by Bandura (1986), which refers to individuals' perceptions about their own abilities to successfully perform a task, and ultimately affects what an individual believes s/he can achieve. In a past review, authors looked at the influence of self-efficacy beliefs on immigrants' life transition (Jerusalem & Mittag, 1997) wherein they had to adapt to various environmental stressors, unemployment, and lack of social support. Jerusalem and Mittag (1997) postulated that individuals with a high sense of efficacy trust their own capabilities and thus tend to master different types of environmental demands. Self-efficacy thus holds evident and critical importance in the present study, as immigrants' self-efficacy will undoubtedly have an influence on their overall transition and retraining experience within Canada, results of post retraining, and career development. Moreover, self-efficacy may have a direct influence on the success of one's general training and learning experience in Canada.

Optimism has received recent attention in the realm of positive psychology, with well known names such as Martin Seligman being a primary researcher behind much of the current research. Optimism can be defined as the tendency to believe that one will experience positive outcomes in life (Lee, Brown, Mitchell, & Schiraldi, 2008), and has been associated with various positive impacts for the individual. Individuals who are seen as optimists tend to live longer, healthier, and happier (Peterson, 2000) lives than those who are not optimists. Furthermore, optimists are considerably more persistent, which makes them more likely to achieve success (Scott, 2011). According to a recent survey, despite some immigrants' dissatisfaction with their current low earnings, they are more optimistic about the future than individuals who are satisfied with their current situation

(Pew Research Centre, 2006). These findings can have important implications for our study, which suggest that despite individual dissatisfaction with their experiences, immigrants held optimistic attitudes. Thus, this suggestion may be indicative of the hope that many immigrants hold, which is an important aspect to be aware of as we explore immigrants' overall optimism and throughout their retraining and career development experience. Given the particular importance of optimism in one's career-life, one's overall optimism levels are expected to have a significant influence on one's transition, training, and overall career development experience.

RATIONALE OF THE STUDY

The purpose of this study was to explore the experience of new immigrant workers in Canada through their engagement in career-related training programs, with particular emphasis on optimism and self-efficacy's influence on various career development elements. The research focused on the subjective learning experience in training programs of workers who were new immigrants to the Greater Toronto Area (GTA), had emigrated to Canada between January 1999 and December 2006, and who had participated in a training program prior to 2008. Therefore, participants in this study had several years to search for a career and to implement their new skills and knowledge that were acquired through the training program.

The central research question in this study was to explore: "How do immigrant retraining programs influence one's overall career development experience in Canada?" Secondary research questions were: (a) What are the immigrants' experiences of self-efficacy and optimism in their overall transition and in relation to their career development? (b) How does one's level of optimism and self-efficacy influence one's relearning experience during the training program? (c) How does one's level of optimism and self-efficacy influence one's post retraining success and content with current work-life situation? The present study sought to uncover key themes from participant narratives through in-depth, phenomenological interviews that attempted to examine immigrant experience in training programs. Through exploration and familiarity of immigrant exposure in training programs, this study aimed to inform: (a) literature within the areas of immigrant transition research, training programs, and relearning, and (b) career counselling, vocational psychology, individual well-being, and studies within the area of new and professional immigrants in Canada. Through the participant narratives, this research aims to generate and provide meaningful knowledge for the aforementioned body of literature and practice, with an overarching goal of contributing to this under-researched area.

The current study is part of a large Canada Research Chair (CRC) project under the direction of Dr. Charles P. Chen. Dr. Chen is the principal investigator (PI) of this project and has several research assistants who are responsible for various aspects of the CRC project, including participant interviews and data analysis. This CRC project explores the overall study of new and professional immigrants' retraining experiences in Canada.

The following chapters explore new and professional immigrant retraining experiences in Canada with a particular focus on immigrant optimism and self-efficacy. Chapter 2 provides an overview of existing literature that focuses on new and professional immigrants' transition and career development. This chapter also outlines barriers and challenges that new immigrants face during their transition to Canada, including cross-cultural barriers, under/unemployment, and stress and health impacts of the transition. In addition, this chapter explores existing literature on immigrant retraining and new learning experiences in Canada. Lastly, this chapter elaborates the potential impact that optimism and self-efficacy have on immigrants' transition and retraining experiences in Canada. Next, chapter 3 outlines the use of a qualitative research methodology within the present study. It discusses the study's use of interviews as a means of gathering meaning and depth from participant narratives and experiences. More specifically, it illustrates the use of a grounded theory approach for this study, alongside the demonstration of the entire research process and all the technical details and procedures involved in the process. Chapter 4 presents the results of the current study. After providing an essential profile of all the research participants, it identified the relevant major themes from the dada analysis based upon participant accounts and viewpoints. In particular, it compares transition and retraining experiences and perspectives among optimistic individuals and pessimistic individuals. Chapter 5 intends to distil and synthesize new knowledge from the primary results of the current study. This chapter discusses the positive impact that optimism had on individuals' transition and retraining experiences, and highlights several components that are associated with optimistic individuals in a career context. Alternatively, it is suggested that pessimistic individuals have an overall more negative transition and retraining experience than their optimistic counterparts. As such, new knowledge from the current study contributes to inform theoretical and conceptual development, professional and self-helping practice, and future research in the realm of immigrant vocational wellness.

Chapter 2

LIFE-CAREERS OF IMMIGRANTS

To facilitate an understanding of the transition and training experience of new and professional immigrants, the main components of the literature and immigrant experience are reviewed in this chapter. These categories include typical transitional difficulties experienced by new immigrants, as well as components of immigrants' psychological well-being. More specifically, this chapter will include research in the area of (a) new and professional immigrants' transitional difficulties, (b) new and professional immigrants' career development, and (c) the influence of immigrants' optimism and self-efficacy on their transition, retraining program, and overall experience. The purpose in exploring these categories is to provide an in-depth perspective of immigrant difficulties after moving to Canada. Lastly, exploration of these categories can provide insight into the potential role that optimism and self-efficacy play in encouraging immigrants to succeed and positively experience their training program.

TRANSITIONAL DIFFICULTIES

New immigrants often face many challenges that coincide with a recent transition to the Canadian societal, economical, and political norms. While these transitional challenges and barriers are vast, research documents the most commonly experienced difficulties for new immigrants to Canada (Dean & Wilson, 2009; Lochhead, 2003; Mak et al., 1994; Reitz, 2001). Among these challenges include an array of cross-cultural difficulties, often leading to difficulties finding and securing a job in one's area of expertise. Resulting from many of these transitional difficulties include a tremendous amount of stress, strain, and burnout symptoms that can become evident in one's physiological and psychological well-being. These transitional difficulties with relation to new and professional immigrants in Canada will be explored in detail in the following section.

CROSS-CULTURAL DIFFICULTIES

As new immigrants transition to Canada, they are confronted with many unforeseen challenges and barriers, related both to their career development and personal experience in Canada. Such difficulties include a myriad of cross-cultural difficulties, including language barriers, adapting from a collectivist society to an individualist society, interpersonal communication differences, and so on. Professional immigrants tend to experience many of the same cross-cultural barriers as non-professional immigrants, despite their additional education/accreditation. In fact, the cross-cultural challenges may be exacerbated for professional immigrants, as they are seeking entry to and advancement in positions requiring highly developed interpersonal communication skills (Mak et al., 1994). Because these difficulties can be experienced both in relation to one's career, as well as being prevalent in one's general activities and routine, these cross-cultural differences pose extreme barriers and frustrations on new immigrants' career development plans.

Language Barriers

All immigrants who are applying to enter Canada under the Federal Skilled Worker Category and the Canadian Experience Class must submit either English or French test results as conclusive proof of English language ability for Citizenship and Immigration Canada (Canada Immigration Lawyers, 2011). These tests include: International English Language Testing System or test d'evaluation francais (English and French, respectively). These tests help Visa Officers determine whether the prospective immigrant has sufficient language ability to enter Canada under the designated class, ultimately allowing for proper integration into the Canadian workforce (Canada Immigration Lawyers, 2011). Even with these assessments and regulations in place, language barriers have been reported as one of the most outstanding difficulties experienced by recent immigrants in Canada. Additionally, 26% of immigrants feel that the English and/or French language remains a significant challenge even four years after their immigration to Canada (Statistics Canada, 2007). Language proficiency is a vital component to a smooth and successful transition into Canada, as virtually all aspects of a transition are highly dependent on communication. Therefore, one must be adept in communicating at all levels, as well as understanding the sheer complexity of the English language, which surpass the demonstration of a specific score on a language test. Not only do new immigrants struggle with the complexity of the English language and consequently experience a difficult job search, but language barriers tend to pose additional problems and misunderstandings for employed immigrants in the workplace (Morris, 2002). Unfortunately, such misunderstandings can sometimes lead to dangerous consequences. For example, a recent study stated that workers whose second language is English are at a significantly higher risk of having an accident on the job as a result of not having a complete grasp of the safety standards (Morris, 2002).

Therefore, while many professional immigrants may have the knowledge, expertise, and experience for a particular career in Canada, research has suggested that immigrants need the proficiency of the English language, an understanding of its complexity, as well as solid communication skills to ease their transition and career development (Morris, 2002; Statistics Canada, 2007).

Transitioning from a Collectivistic to an Individualistic Society

While the nature of cross-cultural barriers are vast, among the most widely experienced cross-cultural difficulty for new immigrants is the transition from a collectivistic to an individualistic society. Individuals from a collectivistic background generally tend to value self-restraint, agreeableness, and modesty (Bond, 1990; King & Bond, 1985; Mak et al., 1994), which can cause confusion, irritation, and frustration when those individuals are required to conform to an individualist society. From a career oriented perspective, a collectivistic society is generally characterized by the individual's tendency to place the organization's needs ahead of their own, portraying a strong sense of loyalty to organizations (Mak et al., 1994). Furthermore, individuals who are part of a collectivistic society generate the majority of their self-worth and career identity from the presence of an amicable relationship with their colleagues (Mak et al., 1994), and define themselves in the context of their connection with others (Rastogi, 2007). Conversely, those persons who have been socialized to individualism place significant emphasis on individual success within the organization, individual achievement, self-actualization, and self-respect (Hofstede, 1984).

The transition from a collectivistic to an individualistic society is a predominantly common stressor due to the influx of immigrants who emigrate from collectivistic societies. China, Philippines, and India are the top three countries that overwhelmingly surpass others in regards to the number of immigrants that immigrate to Canada (Citizenship and Immigration Canada, 2009). Because the majority of immigrants emigrate from these collectively-oriented countries, becoming assimilated with an individualistic society and workplace often poses extreme anxiety and difficulty.

Cross-cultural differences regarding effective communication, interpersonal, and presentational skills can cause extreme anxiety (Gudykunst & Hammer, 1988; Westwood & Ishiyama, 1991) and self-doubt (Zaharna, 1989) in many new minorities, as they are unfamiliar with the host cultural code, both socially and in their work environment (Mak et al., 1994).

In the Canadian society, Westerners are typically individually-driven both in terms of their personal and work lives. For instance, particularly in one's work environment, individuals tend to place their needs and concerns before others, and without consideration of the collective group. Those from an individualist society habitually focus on their own development within their organizational setting. Alternatively, individuals who are raised in a collectivist society are brought up with values that are centered around community, loyalty to organizations, and work from the perspective of team membership (Hofstede, 1984; Mak et al., 1994; Rastogi, 2007). Coming from a collectivistic culture that values agreeableness, teamwork, and harmony, immigrants from such a society often face an extreme culture shock when their Canadian counterparts are seen as self-serving, outspoken, and independent within the workplace (Mak et al., 1994). Therefore, this transition from a collectivist to an individualist society often results in frustration with the Canadian society, its employees, and the hierarchy of organizations. In addition to this frustration comes a significant amount of stress for the individual, which can ultimately lead to a continuous cycle of survival jobs, or difficulty finding suitable employment.

Under/Unemployment

It is at minimum, ironic, that the Canadian government and immigrant policy-makers wish to increase the number of immigrants coming to Canada as a means of filling labour shortages, yet immigrant rates of unemployment are higher than ever before (Camarota & Jensenius, 2009; Statistics Canada, 2007a). These startling rates of immigrant under/unemployment are severely unfortunate when one considers the arduous transition process they must endure. Evidence for the bold unemployment statement lies in the 2006 census, which states that the national unemployment rate for immigrants with a university education was 11.5%, which is more than double the rate of unemployment for the Canadian-born population (Statistics Canada, 2007a). Researchers are seeing that this increased unemployment direction is also a commonality for recent immigrants who have immigrated in 2006 or later. More recently, it has been found that newer immigrants are suffering from detrimental unemployment rates and an overall unfavourable job market, and 13.3% of these immigrants are unemployed (Camarota & Jensenius, 2009). This unemployment rate also seems to be an unfortunate trend with our American counterparts and the state of their immigrants' career development. Not only is immigrant unemployment higher than Native Americans, but research is showing that the most and least educated immigrants in the United States are experiencing the largest increases in unemployment (Camarota & Jensenius, 2009). In fact, for immigrants who had at least a college degree, the unemployment rates increased 6.3% between 2007 and 2009 (Camarota & Jensenius, 2009). The fact that these immigrants are more educated than the native-born population, yet remain unemployed, is a crucial issue that likely adds to the existing stress that immigrants are experiencing.

Among additional stressful pressures experienced by new immigrants is the overall transition period. The transition period is typically referred to as the period after immigrants have come to their new country, are adjusting to new laws and regulations, and are searching for work in their area of expertise. However, because of the extreme stress that is associated with this period, the increases in immigrant unemployment, as well as the ever-increasing length of the transition, some authors have labelled it as the "transition penalty" (Lochhead, 2003, p.1). It is not until 10 years after this period passes that immigrant level of unemployment in Canada falls to the level found among the Canadian-born population (Lochhead, 2003). Therefore, it is understandable as to why some refer to this as a transition penalty, particularly if experiencing under/unemployment for many years. This long transition period, or penalty, constitutes an extreme under-utilization of immigrant skills, where professional immigrants are working survival jobs, simply to be able to financially survive and support themselves and their family. Seeing as the Canadian economy is concerned about labour and skill shortages (Lochhead, 2003), and desires to use immigrant skills as a response to the aging population, it is of critical importance that skill usage and under/unemployment are further explored.

In a metropolitan and diverse city such as Toronto, Canada, we often hear of stories wherein immigrants with university and graduate level education are working as taxi drivers, factory workers, call centre representatives, or in various other survival jobs (Globe and Mail 1996a, 1996b, 1996c, Toronto Star, 1995; Reitz, 2001). These are representative examples of professional immigrants experiencing underemployment, where they are over qualified for their current jobs, but cannot seem to secure a job or career in their qualified area. Underemployment is particularly seen as a waste of quality immigrant skill, knowledge, and expertise (Reitz, 2001). Despite Canadian immigration policy-makers' efforts to upgrade the quality of immigrants entering our country, new and professional immigrants are now more unemployed and underemployed than ever before (Camarota & Jensenius, 2009; Reitz, 2001; Statistics Canada, 2007a). Therefore, despite this rich array of culture, knowledge, and profession making its way into Canada, the knowledge and skills are essentially being wasted, as opposed to being utilized for the benefit of the new immigrants, Canada, and the economy. Consequently, due to the lack of skill utilization, Canada experiences social and political repercussions, in addition to immigrants undergoing numerous associated stress and health impacts (Reitz, 2001).

ASSOCIATED STRESS AND HEALTH IMPACTS

Among the consequences of immigrant under/unemployment include increased poverty rates (Lochhead, 2003), financial strain, as well as an array of many severe physical and psychological stress and strain effects (Dean & Wilson, 2009). Despite the fact that educational attainment of recent immigrant earners has increased significantly faster than their Canadian-born counterparts, earning disparities among recent immigrants and Canadian-born workers continue to exist (Statistics Canada, 2005). In fact, in 1980, recently employed immigrant men earned 85 cents for each dollar received by Canadian-born men; however, by 2005, the ratio had dropped to 63 cents (Statistics Canada, 2005). Similarly, corresponding numbers for recently employed immigrant women were 85 cents and 56 cents, respectively (Statistics Canada, 2005). In addition, about 19% of recent immigrants found themselves in a chronic low income situation, which was defined as having low income for 4 out of 5 years (Statistics Canada, 2007b). The 19% of chronic low-income immigrants is 2.5 times higher than this measurement from the Canadian-born population. Furthermore, the persistency of chronic-low income among immigrants is present, as 16.5% of immigrants identified themselves as being in this category when measured over a ten-year time period (Statistics Canada, 2007b). Accordingly, a significant number of immigrants experience intense levels of stress and consequently experience poor health (Dean & Wilson, 2009; Nidoo, 1992), psychological trauma, as well as unhealthy behaviours, and pathological gambling (Lee, Fong, & Solowoniuk, 2007).

New and professional immigrants in Canada are experiencing an increase in acculturative stress, fear associated with career development, and consequently, a decline in their overall health (Dean & Wilson, 2009). The link between employment and health has been well-documented within recent literature (Dean & Wilson, 2009), and is particularly evident between unemployment and negative physical and psychological health impacts. However, it has only been within recent literature that researchers have included immigrant health as a result of a new transition and regularly associated under/unemployment. For instance, new immigrants in Canada reported experiencing a decline in their mental health as a result of lack of English language skills, under/unemployment, and interfamily conflicts (Jafari et al., 2010).

Given the unique situation of new and skilled immigrants, their health impacts are exacerbated when compared to their immigrant counterparts (Dean & Wilson, 2009). For example, there are particular health concerns associated with de-skilling, wherein immigrants describe a loss of employment-related skills, which is typically accompanied by under/unemployment (Bauder, 2003; Dean & Wilson, 2009). Many immigrants are recognizing that they must maintain their skills acquired through previous education and/or work experience, or their chances of acquiring a job in their field will decrease even further. Accordingly, due to

Life-Careers of Immigrants

these challenges surrounding employment, skill utilization, and associated health impacts, many new and professional immigrants are forced to seek alternative options that will ultimately provide them with an increased chance of employment in their area of expertise.

IMMIGRANT RETRAINING AND NEW LEARNING EXPERIENCES IN CANADA

One particular issue that contributes to immigrant under/unemployment is that some licensing bodies of various trades and professions often do not recognize one's qualifications or credentials that were earned in their host country (Reitz, 2001). In addition, due to the influx of highly educated people immigrating to Canada, retraining is often seen as one of the only avenues within the prevailing condition of limited jobs for educated and qualified specialists (Gorbatova & Eaglstein, 1998). Thus, we see a larger number of new and professional immigrants engaging in training programs, courses, and in educational institutes as a means of learning or enhancing their skills, abilities, and knowledge within a particular area of interest, expertise, or within an area of demand in the job market (Statistics Canada, 2003). There are many reasons why new immigrants engage in training or education programs in Canada; while many immigrants' reasoning's may be due to the previously discussed unemployment situation and difficult labour market, some may enroll as a means of embracing a new opportunity for positive growth and change in a new country, while others may be advised to take further courses or certificate programs by employment counsellors, organizations, or colleagues. Regardless of the rationale and reason behind one's engagement in such a program, it is an increasingly common means of advancement for new immigrants to Canada. In fact, a recent longitudinal survey portrayed that 67% of the immigrant target population planned to get additional training or education after immigrating to Canada (Statistics Canada, 2003). Additionally, although the majority of new immigrants between the ages of 25 to 44 (a prime working age) already had a formal education, 70% of those individuals indicated plans to further pursue education or training (Statistics Canada, 2003). Therefore, the Canadian society and researchers alike are beginning to notice higher education among new immigrants than their Canadian-born counterparts (Statistics Canada, 2008). Despite the fact that increasing numbers of new immigrants are seeking enrollment in training programs and pursuing higher levels of education, researchers have very little insight into the specificities of this retraining and learning experience.

There is an abundance of information to be explored within the context of one's retraining program and new learning experience in Canada. Before researchers can make further developments in the career development process of new and professional immigrants, there must first be an in-depth understanding concerning the conditions and trials of these training experiences. Recent research has, however, made some advancements in the exploration of new immigrants' purpose to pursue training programs or further education (Hongxia, 2009; Shein & Chen, 2011), while other researchers (Beynon, Ilieva, & Dichupa, 2004) have focused on immigrant reaction and expectation to the necessity to engage in retraining in their previously educated careers. In addition, a 2008 study (Cohen-Goldner & Eckstein, 2008) focused on the particular role of training programs on immigrant accumulation of human capital and individual welfare gain. These findings indicated that overall, training programs were highly significant in affecting the labor mobility of immigrants (Cohen-Goldner & Eckstein, 2008). Although this provides support for the effectiveness of such training programs, this study examined these impacts from a quantitative methodology, thus lacking to provide subjective insight into the immigrant training experience. Therefore, there is a paucity of research that truly explores immigrant experience and perspectives throughout this commonly experienced process. Given the increasing popularity of re-educating among this population, it is questionable that more literature hasn't focused on the context of training programs, as well as particular components that are defining of one's overall retraining experience.

INFLUENCE OF IMMIGRANTS' OPTIMISM AND SELF-EFFICACY ON THEIR RETRAINING EXPERIENCE

Optimism and self-efficacy represent two components of individual cognitive style that will be explored within the present study. Individual cognitive style is an important area to consider, as it dictates the way individuals perceive and explain reality, and the ways in which they think about and explain why things happen to them (Kabat-Zinn, 1990). Individuals' optimism and self-efficacy not only helps to explain the rationale behind a good or bad event, but underlies motives for doing things and making choices; optimism and self-efficacy influence the degree of confidence in individuals' ability to make things happen, and serve as a general belief about how the world works, and individuals' place in the world (Kabat-Zinn, 1990).

Understanding individual cognitive style is also an important aspect in career planning and development (Creed, Patton, & Bartrum, 2004). This understanding of cognitive style is meaningful and representative of whether one interprets and experiences events and barriers as a positive opportunity for growth or as being defeating (Creed et al., 2004). Thus, the exploration of optimism and self-efficacy as key cognitive components, and their influence on the transition and career development process of new and professional immigrants is integral. Optimism and self-efficacy were selected as constructs of exploration in this study due to their presumably interconnected relationship within the career development process. Given the influence that one's cognitive style has on one's perception of events, and ultimately, one's experience and actions, it is expected that optimism and self-efficacy will have a significant effect on immigrants' career development experience. Both constructs are key components of psychological well-being, which presumably shape and are affected by one's transition and training experience.

The psychological impact that immigrants experience as a result of their recent transition to a new country has been the focus of many research papers (Dean & Wilson, 2009; Jafari et al., 2010). There are indeed many psychological and physical effects of such a transition, in addition to the impact that a training or education program can have on immigrant health and well-being. However, while previous research has focused on the aversive impacts, the positive impacts of such experiences have not been sufficiently explored. Given the increase of interest in one's attitude on success, happiness, and positive career-related results, it is disconcerting that more theories have not integrated specific components that are telling of one's intent, resiliency, and positive perspective. Therefore, this study aims to gain a holistic understanding of key cognitive components and their influence on the individual's psychological well-being and career development.

OPTIMISM

The forerunner behind optimism is Martin Seligman (1991), who has conducted numerous studies in the area of positive psychology, where he explores the influence of optimism and pessimism on varying events and circumstances. Seligman's (1997) definition of optimism seems to be largely constructed from attribution theory, wherein he refers to people's reasoning for circumstances and events as their explanatory style. For instance, typical optimists have the habit of thinking that bad events are caused by unstable, specific, and external factors, while good events are caused by stable, broad, and internal factors (Segliman & Lee, 1997). Lazarus (1991) also describes optimism/pessimism as a type of appraisal style, as it can influence the way an individual perceives, feels, experiences, and copes with a situation. Given the influence one's explanatory style (tendency to be optimistic or pessimistic) has on various experiences and situations, it is of crucial importance in the present study, where optimism will be explored in relation to one's transition and training experience.

The Health Impacts of Optimism

Literature concerning the impacts of optimism on various aspects of one's life is plentiful. Such literature illustrates one's level of optimism and its impact on quality and length of life, level of stress, level of success, and so on. Scott (2011) found that aside from experiencing less stress than both pessimists and realists, optimists live significantly longer, have a higher level of emotional health, and are thus more likely to achieve success. Furthermore, in their 2002 study, Creed, Patton, and Bartrum discovered that those individuals who had high levels of optimism also reported high levels of self-esteem and low levels of psychological distress, whereas pessimists' levels of self-esteem and psychological distress were reversed. Optimism's positive influence on health has even been researched and portrayed in regards to cancer treatment and survival (Scott, 2011), suggesting optimism's significant impact on well-being. Overall, the influence of optimism on one's health has been successfully represented within the Western population (Creed et al., 2002; Scott, 2011); however, such literature has not examined optimism's health impacts on new immigrants. Research that explores the relationship between immigrant optimism and health can provide preliminary literature for new and professional immigrants. Because the literature has thus far documented the harsh costs associated with the immigrant transition period, assuaging related stress is of crucial importance to easing the transition period, and to the overall betterment of new immigrants. Despite the paucity of research in regards to immigrant optimism and health, research has recently included optimism as an increasingly researched component in association with career development.

Optimism and Career Development

Recent studies examining the role of career development have also been suggesting optimism as a vital role in one's transition and overall career development process (Creed et al., 2002; Kaniel, Massey, & Robinson,

2010). Despite the fact that there have only been a few studies that have investigated optimism within vocational psychology, these studies have produced striking findings. This optimism and career literature supports the direction of these career development studies and their association with optimism as a key psychological tenet. A recent study (Kaniel et al., 2010) examined the optimistic disposition on MBA students' job searches and initial phase of their career development. This study found that optimists not only landed a job more easily and with less effort, but were more likely than their non-optimistic counterparts to be promoted just two years after graduation (Kaniel et al., 2010). Furthermore, Creed et al. (2002) examined effects of optimism and pessimism on career variables and components of well-being, and found that individuals who had high optimism scores also reported high levels of career planning and exploration, had a higher sense of confidence and career maturity about their career-related decisions, and had more career related goals than pessimists. Alternatively, pessimists displayed more career indecisiveness, had lower levels of decision-making knowledge, and reported lower levels of achievement than optimists (Creed et al., 2002). Additionally, Patton, Bartrum, and Creed (2002) found support for a career development model wherein optimism and career locus of control were predictive of career planning and career exploration amongst various barriers, unexpected job-related variables, and career goals. Although the relationship between optimism and career development has seen an increasing amount of literature within recent years, it has not been applied in sufficient manner to the career development needs, barriers, retraining/education programs, and experiences of new and professional immigrants. Optimism and immigrant career development has the potential to serve as a very powerful relationship, given the significant findings linking optimism and various components of career development. While immigrant optimism and career development has yet to be examined, recent literature has integrated optimism as a psychological component in regards to immigrant transitions, which is outlined in the following section.

The Influence of Optimism on Immigrant Transitions

Given the particularly difficult transition that new and professional immigrants undergo, one would expect their stress, mental and physical health, and general attitude to be aversely impacted. However, while new immigrants' stress and health (Dean & Wilson, 2009; Jafari, 2008) seem to be impacted during the transition to a new country, their sense of optimism appears to flourish. A recent study examined particular ethnic groups of immigrants within the United States of America, and found that 39% of immigrants identified as earning below $15,000 per year, which qualifies them as being significantly below the poverty threshold (Ruiz, 2010). Despite this extremely low financial situation, 74% of these individuals stated that they would still have made the choice to immigrate to their new country, and that they see this as an opportunity to flourish and do better (Ruiz, 2010). These findings are striking, as one may argue that these individuals are in the most detrimental and disadvantaged situations in the country, yet somehow remain to be optimistic about their future. In an additional study that explored Korean immigrants and their current hardships, optimism was significantly correlated to immigrants' resilience (Lee et al., 2008). Resilience has been defined by Amundson, Borgen, and Reuter (2004) as "one's ability to overcome or adapt to a stressful situation" (p. 51). In addition, Hagevik (1998) described a link between optimism and career resilience, suggesting that individuals must have an optimistic attitude that characterizes the ability to be flexible and proactive. Lee et al. (2008) suggested that optimism be further explored as a key psychological component that likely increases the chance of developing career resiliency.

Optimism was also examined as a primary component in Albanian immigrants' ability to adapt and cope with the 1999 Kosovo crisis after immigrating to the United States (Riolli, Savicki, & Cepani, 2002). Specifically, the participants in this study showed that due to their increase in stress, reduced optimism was related to maladjustment (Riolli et al., 2002). Riolli et al. (2002) also confirmed support for the positive influence of optimism's presence, wherein those immigrants with higher levels of optimism also had higher resiliency in the face of these traumatic stress conditions. Optimism has been seen as a key tenet throughout the face of distress and misfortunes as optimists appear to possess the ability to persevere in the face of initial adversity (Rasmussen, Wrosch, Scheier, & Carver, 2006). The sense of well-being that stems from a deeply held conviction that the future will turn out favourably may allow optimists to adapt more flexibly and effectively to changes and hardships that they experience (Rasmussen et al., 2006). Given optimists' likelihood to thrive and excel within various circumstances and amidst many hardships, its applicability as an integral facet to immigrants' transition and retraining experience deems exploring. Because immigrants experience such a difficult transition period, their resilience and optimism are presumed to play a significant role in their overall well-being, in addition to the nature of their transition and retraining experience in Canada.

SELF-EFFICACY

An additional cognitive component that has received significant attention in relation to career development is self-efficacy. Its represented relation and popularity to career development theories (Betz, 2000; Betz & Hackett, 1981) deems this component worthy of further attention. Self-efficacy, defined as the individuals' views of their ability to organize and take action to successfully attain the desired results (Bandura, 1986), has been a main component in career theories since 1980 (Betz, 2000; Betz & Hackett, 1981), and has since been thriving within recent literature. The concept and role of self-efficacy in one's career development has become increasingly important in predicting numerous career-related variables, with much of this attention being largely due to Bandura's social cognitive theory (1986), which evolved into Lent, Brown, and Hackett's social cognitive career theory (1993). In fact, self-efficacy is seen as the main component in social cognitive career theory, as it plays a key role in the prediction of one's career development process. Self-efficacy also portrays a significant role in career decision making, as it affects how individuals view their capabilities and skills, and what they believe they are able to achieve (Sharf, 2010). Self efficacy is, therefore, within a similar framework as self-esteem, but is more so applied to one's belief about his/her abilities in regards to a particular task, as opposed to a perception of oneself. This self-efficacy perception of one's own capabilities thus affects academic and career choices, ultimately influencing the overall career development process. For example, individuals with a low sense of self-efficacy will likely believe they are not capable of successfully performing a particular task, and will in turn have a difficult time pursuing and achieving their career-related goals. Alternatively, individuals with a high sense of self-efficacy are less troubled and less likely to be overwhelmed by perceived challenges and barriers, and will be more likely to use these circumstances as positive opportunities for growth. Therefore, such individuals have a higher perception of their abilities and skills and in turn, believe there is a higher likelihood that they will succeed with career-related skills and goals.

In 1981, it was proposed that career self-efficacy played a more powerful role than that of interests, values, and actual abilities (Hackett & Betz, 1981) in regards to career choice and development. Such persuasive support for self-efficacy has continued to serve as a primary representation in studies replicating and strengthening its role (Betz, 2000). For instance, one's efficacy beliefs exert a strong and direct influence on career decision making, career choice, as well as being significantly integral to the development of key vocational choice predictors (Bandura, 1986; Betz, 2000; Hackett & Lent, 1992). Furthermore, self-efficacy has also been shown to be related to one's leadership behaviour in a career setting, particularly portraying a relationship between a high sense of self-efficacy and leadership behaviours (Schyns, 2001; Shea & Howell, 1999).

In more recent research, Lent (2005) suggested that self-efficacy that is slightly greater than one's true skills and abilities may be useful in further skill development and motivation, while Creed et al. (2004) determined that self-efficacy was predictive of career planning and development, and that higher levels of self-esteem was associated with more decision-making self-efficacy. More specifically, self-efficacy was predictive of career development attitude, career development knowledge, and career indecision (Creed et al., 2004). Schyns (2004) discusses the importance of self-efficacy on organizations and suggests that if such organizations plan to implement changes or are in the midst of change processes, they should pay particular attention to their employees' levels of self-efficacy. Such individual efficacy can be representative of successful leaders or employees within the organization. This suggestion marks the importance of self-efficacy as a crucial component in training programs, as individuals engaged in such programs are also in the midst of change processes. Therefore, by becoming aware of immigrant efficacy levels, researchers will be better able to further understand immigrant cognitive style and its impact on the individual's future career development.

While these studies focused on the role of self-efficacy in what is primarily a career oriented framework, much research has also focused on self-efficacy in the context of educational and university settings, providing merit to the role of self-efficacy in a learning environment (Adachi, 2001; Chang, 2006; Gushue, 2006; Gushue & Whitson, 2006). Therefore, understanding individuals' sense of self-efficacy can serve as a significant predictor of their overall success and attitude within such training programs. While the majority of the present self-efficacy research has consisted of the use of primarily caucasian individuals, recent research has made efforts to explore self-efficacy in regard to diverse populations.

The Role of Immigrant Self-Efficacy

While few studies have examined the link between self-efficacy and career development within the professional immigrant population, several studies have explored such a relationship among diverse populations, including ethnic minorities. Although new immigrants and ethnic minorities undoubtedly vary, the present studies provide relevant information for a link between self-efficacy and career development among diverse populations. For instance, Adachi (2001) reported that self-efficacy had an impact on Japanese college students' intentions to explore occupations, while Chang (2006) reported similar findings with a population of Korean American women. While it is transparent that self-efficacy exists in relation to diverse populations and their career development, the level of efficacy beliefs in an ethnic minority seem to differ from that of a typical North American individual. For example, Luzzo and McWhirter (2001) reported that ethnic minorities believed they had lower levels of self-efficacy for coping with career related barriers than their European American counterparts. A number of authors supported this finding (Weiss, 2001; Klassen, 2004), while Weiss (2001) stated that the greater the perceived likelihood of career barriers and challenges, the lower the career self-efficacy among various diverse populations, including African American and Asian American individuals.

While the majority of recent studies have focused on efficacy and career development among diverse populations, some authors have focused attention on the immigrant population. Jerusalem and Mittag (1995), for instance, explored levels of self-efficacy in stressful life transitions among new immigrants. In particular, they reported that perceived self-efficacy had significant effects on perceived threat, loss, and challenge appraisal (the extent to which one views transitional stressors as challenging in a positive manner, or as a negative appraisal). More specifically, those with low perceived efficacy felt more threatened than those with high efficacy beliefs, while those immigrants with the highest efficacy beliefs benefitted substantially and experienced the most favourable adaptation process (Jerusalem & Mittag, 1995). Jerusalem and Mittag's (1995) study provides significant meaning for the present study, as it implies that self-efficacy plays a meaningful role in the adaptation process of new immigrants. In addition, Klassen (2004) examined several reviews and found interesting findings relevant to both the ethnic minority and immigrant populations. For instance, efficacy beliefs of a cultural group were found to be modified through immigration or political changes (Klassen, 2004), which posits important considerations for the present study. What also strikes as relevant to the present literature is that efficacy beliefs and performance appeared to be strengthened when training approaches were congruent with the individual's sense of self (Klassen, 2004). The aforementioned studies illustrate the important role that efficacy holds in both the immigrant transition and training experience, in addition to the role that the transition and training process have on one's efficacy beliefs. Therefore, this study plans to explore self-efficacy's role within new and professional immigrants' transition to Canada, their training program, and overall career development.

While current literature is expanding its participant population to allow for better representation across Canada, literature has yet to qualitatively explore the role of self-efficacy on new and professional immigrants in a training or education program. A retraining or education program has unique factors that are not present within a transition experience to a new country, and will likely invoke different feelings, perceptions, and experiences than that of a typical transition process. Towards this end, the current research seeks to use immigrant narratives of their transition experience to Canada, education or reaccreditation experience in Canada. Furthermore, it intends to provide insight into how the roles of optimism and self-efficacy influenced their perception and experience in such programs, and in their overall career development experience.

OPTIMISM, SELF-EFFICACY, AND RETRAINING

While there are numerous components and variables that inevitably influence immigrants' experience in a training program, optimism and self-efficacy are the primary focus of the present study for several reasons. Firstly, as noted in the aforementioned sections, researchers (Creed et al., 2004; Kaniel, Massey, & Robinson, 2010; Klassen, 2004; Lee et al., 2008; MIT Sloan Management Review, 2010; Schyns, 2004; Weiss, 2001) are increasingly identifying the importance of both optimism and self-efficacy beliefs within the career development literature. While the importance of these variables have been identified with many populations, their influence on immigrants' transition and training experience has been under explored. Of those studies that have examined the impact of optimism and self-efficacy on immigrants' transition and career development, their findings provide strong support for the roles of optimism and efficacy beliefs within the immigrant population. More particularly, a review of studies (Klassen, 2004) have supported claims that efficacy beliefs are modified throughout immigrants' transition to a new country, while Riolli et al.'s (2002) study found that immigrants with higher optimism levels were better able to cope with traumatic stress. Recent research has made many strides in the realm of optimism, efficacy beliefs, and career development, however, these components have not yet been collaboratively and qualitatively explored in the professional immigrant population; therefore, this study plans to examine the interrelatedness of optimism, efficacy beliefs, and immigrants' transition and training experience.

Chapter 3

RESEARCH PROCESS

The current study utilized a qualitative research approach, which included in-depth interviews designed to gather narrative data and the grounded theory approach to analyze this data. This research methodology was chosen as a means to gain a comprehensive understanding of new and professional immigrants' transitions, career development experiences, as well as their experiences and perspectives on training programs in Canada. This chapter details the rationale for use of a qualitative design and details the grounded theory approach. The methodology of this study is outlined and includes a description of procedures used for recruitment and selection of participants, a detailed description of the interview process, along with participant characteristics, and procedures for data collection and analysis.

RATIONALE FOR QUALITATIVE DESIGN

A qualitative methodology was chosen for the present study as a means of gathering in-depth and detailed narratives that would not be present in a quantitative study. Qualitative methods allow for greater understanding and access to participant narratives and experiences than are present in observation and quantification. Many researchers advocate the importance of qualitative studies with specific attention to the role of the participant. For example, while participants are generally seen as objects in quantitative studies, they play a primary role in qualitative studies, and are generally seen as subjects, experts, and informants, as they are the providers of such information (Grace, 2011; Outwaithe, 1986). Additionally, qualitative methodologies help researchers gain access to underlying feelings, meanings, perspectives, ideologies, and consequences that are present and seen as primary components to the participants' experience (Thompson, 1981).

Despite psychology's past reliance on quantitative methodologies, many researchers are shifting to the use of qualitative methodologies, particularly in counselling psychology (Ponterotto, 2005). Such a shift is likely due to the abundance of information that is absent within quantitative designs, as qualitative designs serve to broaden our intellectual perspectives and findings through the use of an exploratory method (Ponterotto, 2005). This perspective has been supported within many different realms of psychology, including career and vocational psychology (Chen, 2006; Chen & Lee, 2011; Cochran, 1990; Shein & Chen, 2010). Due to the ever-evolving nature of one's career, to solely measure, control, and quantify career-related variables would be to overlook an adequate array of rich literature. The exploration of one's career is not only a picture of his/her job, but delves into many other aspects of the individual's life. As Cochran (1990) states, "A career includes life roles generally as they rise and fall in a person's pattern of self-development" (p.4). Therefore, we see the importance in the use of qualitative methodologies in regards to one's career experience.

Immigrant career transition and learning experiences in Canada demand further qualitative exploration. Given the nature of the interviews employed by the present study and the broad range of possible information, it is pertinent that this study used qualitative methodologies as the primary means in the exploration of immigrant career transition and learning experiences. Additionally, because this study examined components such as self-efficacy and optimism, qualitative methodologies will allow for further depth than that of a quantitative study. From this standpoint, researchers were able to take a perspective that focuses on the unique understanding of each individual story. Participants were therefore given the opportunity to openly share their entire experience, including details about their transition, job-search in Canada, nature of the retraining program, and their post retraining experience. Such participant perspective consists of a broad range of aspects, including participant cognition, affect, intentions, and so on (Maxwell, 2005). Therefore, we are not solely focused on objective physical events and behaviours, but how the participants make sense of these, and how this understanding influences their decisions (Maxwell, 2005), and ultimately, their career path. Furthermore, implementing this design will allow us to understand how events, actions, and meanings are shaped by unique circumstances (Maxwell, 2005), and the process through which participants derive personal meaning from such events and circumstances. In the present study, participants were able to divulge such personal information while researchers focused specific attention to particular themes and concepts that may not have been accounted for in an objective approach.

It is for these reasons, along with the significant amount of literature supporting such research, that this study implemented a qualitative methodology. This phenomenological study utilized data gathered via narrative interviews to discover new and professional immigrants' experience transitioning to Canada, as well as their retraining and post-retraining experience. Furthermore, this study explored how their individual optimism and self-efficacy influenced their retraining and post-retraining experience in their career. A grounded theory approach was employed as the primary means of organizing and analyzing the gathered data.

A Grounded Theory Approach

A grounded theory methodology is grounded in its approach through the use of data, which is gathered from semi-structured phenomenological interviews. Glaser (1999) stated that "grounded theory tells us what is going on, tells us how we can account for the participants' main concerns, and reveals access variables that account for incremental change" (p.836).

Because this study plans to uncover such information, grounded theory was deemed an appropriate methodology to implement in the present study.

Grounded theory derives its theoretical foundation from Pragmatism (Dewey, 1925; Mead, 1934) and Symbolic Interactionism (Blumer, 1969; Corbin & Strauss, 1990; Hughes, 1971; Park & Burgess, 1921). Grounded theory was developed by Glaser and Strauss in 1967 when quantitative methodology was gaining strides within various areas of research (Charmaz & Mitchell, 1996). Glaser and Strauss (1967) developed systematic methodological approaches in many different research topics, and advocated that researchers develop themes and findings from the data, rather than forming preconceived hypotheses. Therefore, grounded theory became known for advocating the importance in remaining open to unique participant experiences before conceptualizing a research direction (Glaser & Strauss, 1967).

Grounded theory soon evolved during the late 1980's and early 1990's. The evolution of grounded theory can be characterized by many factors. For instance, the two original authors of grounded theory built divergent approaches to their own method, where they cited procedural and rigorous guidelines as primary components of grounded theory (Charmaz & Mitchell, 1996). However, more recent researchers (Bryant, 2002; Charmaz, 2006; Clarke, 2005; Seale, 1999) have re-conceptualized grounded theory to take more modern methodological approaches into account. Their research has resulted in a division in grounded methodology approaches: constructivist and objectivist grounded theory. The former is reflective of interpretive tradition, while objectivist grounded theory results from positivism (Bryant, 2002; Clarke, 2005). Moreover, such evolution and reflexive grounded theory approaches allow for "twenty first century methodological assumptions" within the present study (Charmaz, 2006, p.9).

The nature in implementing a grounded theory approach allows the current researcher to identify unanticipated phenomena, meanings, and influences, and to generate grounded theories about such influences (Maxwell, 2005). Because the present study is exploring ever-changing variables throughout immigrant transition and training experiences, it is important to incorporate an approach that values such meaningful

Research Process

adjustment. This perspective is shared by Corbin and Strauss (1990), where they state that "since phenomena are not conceived of as static but as continually changing in response to prevailing conditions, an important component of the method is to build change, through process, into the method" (p.419). This study will therefore, implement a grounded approach that will be representative of change.

Through this process of exploration, grounded theory will help the present researcher to derive not only meanings and themes, but will help uncover the participant's reaction to such conditions and circumstances (Corbin & Strauss, 1990). After deriving such interpretations, the researcher is able to compile participant narratives into various categories, ultimately determining the prominent themes that were evident throughout participant narratives. After identifying emerging categories which will be derived from the data, the researcher can then construct responses to the primary questions of the present study.

PROCEDURES

Recruitment

Participants for this study were recruited through the use of poster advertisements in the Toronto Transit Commission (TTC) and through the use of online advertisements. Recruitment was also facilitated through snowball sampling, as participants shared information about the study through word of mouth. The advertisements detailed the purposes of the study, the selection criteria for participation, and contact information. Recruitment took place over a period of 4 months.

Selection Criteria

The targeted sample for this study were new and professional Canadian immigrant workers. More specifically, they were immigrants in the Toronto or Greater Toronto Areas (GTA) who: (1) were not born in Canada, (2) immigrated to Canada between the years of January 1, 1999 to December 30, 2006, (3) were at least 25 years of age or older on the date of the interview, (4) have a university degree that was earned outside of Canada, (5) worked full-time in a professional occupation in their country of origin for at least three years before coming to Canada, (6) engaged in retraining in Canada and earned a university, college or professionally certified and formal diploma, certificate, certification or accreditation (proof of this record was required to participate in the interviews), (7) have held employment in Canada (part-time or full-time) for a minimum of 1 year after completing the Canadian retraining, (8) were fluent in English, and (9) have not previously participated in any of Dr. Charles P. Chen's research projects to date.

The first two criteria were put in place to ensure that the participants were newcomers to Canada, and to help ensure that they had adequate time to look for employment, engage in a training program, and to hold employment for one year post-retraining. The third criterion was present to ensure that participants were of age to have had proper experience within their area of employment. The fourth and fifth criteria were included to ensure that the participants were accredited professional individuals in their area of expertise and that they had sufficient employment experience within this field before immigrating to Canada. The sixth and seventh criteria were put in place to ensure that the participants had professional retraining experience in Canada, and held subsequent training employment experience, both of which we will be able to explore. The eighth criterion was present to allow for in-depth interviews, as the interviews were being conducted in English. Additionally, it is presumed that the experience of those individuals who are fluent in English would be fundamentally different from those individuals who are not able to speak fluent English. Due to the available resources and rationale for the present study, the latter individuals were not able to be included. Lastly, the ninth criterion was present to ensure that Dr. Charles P. Chen's studies do not contain duplicate information.

Research Interviews/Data Collection

Potential participants responded by telephone or email to the advertisements posted on the TTC or the online services. Individuals were contacted by telephone to determine their willingness to participate and to ensure that they fit all of the selection criteria. A written telephone script was used by the researchers in an effort to ensure various details about the nature and purpose of the study, selection criteria, confidentiality, reimbursement, length of interview, and additional matters, in an effort to remain standardized and to provide consistency to the potential participants. During the initial selection process, participants were cautioned of the possible distressing impacts they may experience as a result of the interview, but were told that they would hopefully find this process to be cathartic and an overall positive experience in relation to their career development process. Options for support in the form of referrals, psychological assistance, and crisis lines were readily available for participants in the event that they found the experience of re-telling their personal stories pre-Canada, their transition, and re-training and post-retraining experiences difficult or very distressing. Participants were reminded that their employer would have no knowledge of their participation in this study, and were also assured that they were free to withdraw from the interview and the current research project at any time without penalty. During the initial contact via the telephone, interview times were scheduled.

Interviews were conducted in private rooms in the OISE Psychoeducational and Counselling Clinic at the University of Toronto. Interview sessions were approximately 1.5-2 hours in length and were audio-taped. Each participant was compensated for their time in the amount of $35 per interview. To ensure confidentiality, all research materials were kept in Dr. Charles P. Chen's locked research office, in a locked filing cabinet, to which only the researchers and Dr. Charles P. Chen had access. At the beginning of each interview, researchers reminded the participants about the nature and content of the study, limits of confidentiality, and anonymity. Participants signed an informed consent sheet which included such details about the study, and also gave consent that the interview would be audio-taped for transcribing purposes only. At the end of the interview, participants were provided with their compensation fee, and accordingly signed an information sheet detailing their receipt of this fee.

A phenomenological interview detailed a narrative description of each participant's life-career transition and retraining experience in Canada. There were 76 interview questions that participants were asked. Such questions included those which focused on various times in the participant's life and career. More specifically, the questions were divided into the following categories: (1) before coming to Canada, (2) after coming to Canada (initial general experience), (3) ongoing vocational adjustment and transition in Canada, (4) plans for and engagement in retraining program, (5) results of post re-training, and (6) current employment. Specific questions that focused on immigrant optimism and self-efficacy include: (1) Before coming to Canada: How central was your career to your sense of self?, (2) How confident did you feel about finding work in your profession?, (3) What were your expectations of the retraining process? What did you think the experience would be like?, (4) After coming to Canada: How did your ability to cope with changes impact your self-esteem and confidence levels?, (5) Ongoing vocational adjustment and transition in Canada: Thinking about your pre-Canada skills and abilities, how did you think you would perform in the retraining?, (6) How did you feel about having to take this retraining? (i.e., resentment for the necessity of retraining vs. framing it as a new opportunity and positive chance for growth), (7) Results of post-retraining: How did you feel about your skills and abilities after the training program?, (8) Current employment: Have any factors challenged your beliefs that you could succeed in your career/work life?, and (9) How satisfied do you feel about your career/work-life experience in Canada? Additional questions that focused on immigrant attitude and perspectives included: 10) Considering your life as it has turned out until now, how much of an element of choice has there been? Is the job you do a chosen vocation or more or less the result of a series of chance events? Are there any aspects of your life that are the result of a considered choice?, and 11) What has the role of chance been in your life and career in Canada? What did you do in response to chance events? These questions are deemed closely related to

Research Process   39

the overall research questions that have been investigated in the present study. The questions provide insight into participants' attitudes and their levels of optimism and self-efficacy. Finally, the questions give an overall understanding of new and professional immigrants' Canadian retraining and career development experience.

Participant Characteristics

The present study consisted of 7 males and 3 females. The average age of all 10 participants was 44.3 years, with a range of 29 to 64 years. The average age of male participants was 44.5 years, with a range of 29 to 64 years. The average range of female participants was 43.6 years, with a range of 36 to 53 years. The present study did not place requirements on the status of individuals, and therefore included both married and single participants. In addition, many of the participants had children, with a range of 0 to 3 children per family. In terms of cultural backgrounds and countries of origin, six participants were from Asia (China, Yemen, Philippines, and 3 participants from India), two participants were from Europe (Ukraine), one participant was from the United States of America, and one participant was from Africa (Kenya). The highest level of education completed pre-Canada was a Masters degree for two of the female participants, while the remaining eight participants had undergraduate university degrees. One of the participants spoke English as his mother language.

Data Analysis

The initial stage of data analysis involved an in-depth reading of the participant narratives. After each transcript was read, line by line analysis was done in an effort to highlight and code provisional themes that appeared evident throughout each narrative. This analyzing and coding was done through the use of NVivo 8, the open coding of data into multiple categories (Strauss & Corbin, 1990). Annotations and notes were made throughout the process in an effort to make note of any potential or significant category or theme. Each transcript was analyzed and coded multiple times in an effort to highlight areas of relevance to the participants' career development within Canada. Furthermore, highlighting key themes within the realm of optimism and self-efficacy beliefs in regard to participants' transition and training experience was prioritized. The data was again studied and reduced through implementation of grounded theory methodology. After such, saturation was achieved and key categories, themes, and subcategories emerged.

ORGANIZATION AND PRESENTATION OF THE FINDINGS

As the final part of the data analysis, the research findings were organized into two primary sections. The first section is titled Optimism, which details participants' general level of optimism amidst various challenges, optimism throughout and post-retraining program, and their levels of optimism in relation to their career-life outcome. Within this section includes participants' identification of attitude as being important. Lastly, this section details experiences of those participants whose optimism decreased as a result of various challenges and barriers. The second section is titled Efficacy beliefs and explores participants' levels of self-efficacy and beliefs in regards to their career skills and abilities before, during, and after their retraining program. These sections will provide readers with information on any possible change or fluctuation throughout each participant's experience and may give some indication as to possible factors that may have attributed to this change in attitude. Each section will include an overall perspective of participants' personal and career development experience within Canada and their retraining/education program. Lastly, additional themes that arose within the data analysis yet fell outside the realm of this study's original area of interest will be presented. The following chapter will begin with a brief introduction of each participant before presenting the two primary sections and corresponding components that emerged within the data analysis.

Chapter 4

Life-Career Themes

The present chapter first provides a brief profile of each participant. In particular, it details their education and career life before coming to Canada and their career development experience in Canada, including the nature of their retraining program and post-retraining employment. Key themes related to the experiences of immigration, overall transition, and retraining were generated and organized into two major themes: Optimism and Self-Efficacy. From here, optimism was further constructed into two categories: Optimists and Pessimists, where participants were classified based on their levels of optimism and pessimism. The present researcher also identified some participants as having neutral attitudes. These participants did not have explicitly positive or negative views, but seemed to fluctuate quite naturally and changed their perspectives and attitudes based on their experiences. Neutralists' experiences and narratives are therefore provided within both sections. The organization of these categories allows for key comparisons to be made between optimists' and pessimists' transition and retraining experiences. Lastly, participants' self-efficacy at various times throughout their immigration, transition, and retraining experience is discussed.

Participant 1

Participant 1 (P1) is a 41-year-old man who emigrated from China in March of 2005 when he was 34 years of age. He attended university in his home country and received his Bachelor's degree in Electrical Engineering. Prior to immigrating to Canada, P1 was employed as an electrical engineer, and made the decision to immigrate to Canada due to his impression of Canada's economic growth and its potential for economic development.

P1 describes his experience finding survival jobs as being "very easy" (P1), and worked several of these before taking a training program which focused on automotive technology. P1 states that he chose this training program due to a personal interest, stating "...in Canada you must drive a car, and I'd better like to know, not focusing on the job, but if you drive you'd better know what's wrong with your car, so that's why I'm choosing that course." Shortly after P1 completed this course, he became employed with the TTC, which was his desired job when he initially came to Canada.

Participant 2

Participant 2 (P2) is a 53-year-old woman who emigrated from Kenya in 2001 when she was 42 years of age. P2 immigrated to Canada with her husband and 2 sons. She attended a 3-year university program in Kenya and has a diploma in computers and executive assistant, which is the highest secretarial group. Before immigrating to Canada, P2 was employed in the private sector and was a senior executive assistant to the chairman of an international company. She was very happy in her job, but stated that "there wasn't too much opportunity to come up...to develop" (P2).

P2 immigrated to Canada in the hopes of providing a better life and future for her children, due to some of the dangers and crimes that occur in Kenya. P2 had a very positive transition to Canada, describing that her family is very strong minded and adjusts to changes very fast, claiming that they have a very positive attitude. When she arrived to Canada, P2 sought employment in a temporary position with the same international company

Life-Career Themes 43

that she worked for in Kenya, and soon after moved to a second job, which was similar in nature. P2 was motivated to pursue a training program, as she has always wanted to further her education, and the opportunity was present for her in Canada. She decided to pursue her Law Clerk diploma at Centennial College approximately 5 years after she arrived in Canada. Following the completion of her program, she applied for and received her current job within the same company, which has more relation to her retraining courses.

Participant 3

Participant 3 (P3) is a 39-year-old male who emigrated from Ukraine in 2001 when he was 28 years of age. P3 did not immigrate to Canada with any family members or friends. He holds a Bachelor of Finance from a university in Ukraine, a Master's degree in Economics, and has also completed several courses from an MBA program in the United States. Before coming to Canada, P3 states that he was professionally satisfied with his job as an investment analyst, but was not personally satisfied, due to his financial income.

P3 was encouraged to immigrate to Canada because he believed there would be significant opportunity for employment within his field. P3 had a very difficult transition to Canada, particularly in terms of finding a job within his field. He anticipated having to take a retraining program after arriving in Canada, and completed several Canadian Securities courses. While P3 describes the courses as being required and therefore useful to his employment opportunities, he is not satisfied in his current role as a financial analyst.

Participant 4

Participant 4 (P4) is a 29-year-old male who emigrated from India in November of 2005 when he was 22 years of age. P4 completed a Bachelor in Electrical Engineering in India and was subsequently employed as an equity dealer. He was extremely satisfied with his job before moving to Canada, and states that his rationale for coming to Canada was due to discordance between his education (Electrical Engineering) and his interests (Finance). Therefore, he felt that he had more freedom in terms of enrolling in financial programs and courses in Canada. In addition, his girlfriend resided in Canada, which also solidified his decision to immigrate to Canada.

P4 had a relatively difficult transition to Canada, mainly because he was only given a temporary visa, which prohibited him from working, resulting in being unemployed for 3 years. Therefore, he immediately decided to pursue retraining in Canada, in an effort to provide proof of Canadian certification to potential employers and increase his probability in securing a job in his field. P4 pursued his Canadian education at the Canadian Securities Institute, where he completed a Derivatives Fundamental course. P4 is currently employed in 2 jobs; one being a temporary job within his area of interest, while the other job is present to simply keep busy.

Participant 5

Participant 5 (P5) is a 64-year-old male who emigrated from Yemen with his wife and 2 children in August 2000 when he was 52 years of age. He completed a Bachelor of Science in Electrical Engineering from a university in the United Kingdom (UK). Before coming to Canada, P5 was employed as a Training Manager in Yemen and was relatively content with his job; however, he was not satisfied with the level of pay.

P5 was motivated to come to Canada for the well-being and consideration of his children, as they would have had little rights within Yemen. P5 describes his family's transition to Canada as being positive in nature, but further notes that his biggest difficulty was the low salary in his initial survival jobs. After P5's son was accepted into a university program, P5 was then encouraged to also apply for his Bachelor of Arts degree, as he describes himself as having been stuck in his previous survival job. Since coming to Canada, P5 has completed his Bachelor of Arts with a major in

Political Science. Additionally, he is currently completing a Master's degree in Political Science and is employed as a teaching assistant at a university in Ontario.

Participant 6

Participant 6 (P6) is a 36-year-old female who emigrated from Ukraine in October 2002 with her husband when she was 26 years old. She has completed a Master of Arts degree with a concentration in English language and World Literature. Before immigrating to Canada, she was employed in a non-governmental organization as a Consultant. She was extremely satisfied with this career, and immigrated to Canada primarily due to her husband's career change.

P6 decided to pursue further education after she was not accepted for particular jobs, and was having an unsuccessful experience with the application process. P6 therefore applied and was accepted to a university in Ontario where she completed her Master of Business Administration (MBA). Upon completion of this degree, P6 was successful in finding employment with a strategic consulting firm.

Participant 7

Participant 7 (P7) is a 42-year-old male who emigrated from the United States in 2003 to live with his wife when he was 33 years of age. P7 completed a Bachelor of Arts degree with a concentration in Chemistry in the United States and was employed as a chemist before immigrating to Canada. He was also previously enrolled in a Master of Social Work (MSW) program in the United States, but did not continue pursuing this degree due to financial reasons. P7 had a difficult transition to Canada which was primarily due to career-related hardships, particularly in terms of securing a job appropriate to his education and skills.

Shortly after his transition, P7 decided that he should obtain some Canadian education as a means of alleviating his career-related difficulties. Therefore, he decided to enroll in a Certified General Accountant (CGA) program. Soon after completing and working as a CGA for a few years, P7 applied and was accepted to a Teacher Education program at the Ontario Institute for Studies in Education (OISE). In addition to his teaching diploma, P7 enrolled in online Advanced Qualification (AQ) courses pertaining to his teaching and accounting designations. P7 is presently employed as an instructor and is content with his current position. In addition to P7's pre-Canada Bachelor of Arts degree, his Canadian CGA designation, and Bachelor of Education, he has also completed a Canadian Securities course, and at the time of this interview, was enrolled in a Real Estate course. He shared that he enjoys the process of retraining and reeducating himself, stating that he "is never going to stop."

Participant 8

Participant 8 (P8) is a 52-year-old Indian male who immigrated to Canada in 2002 with his wife and son when he was 42 years of age. His pre-Canada education includes a Bachelor of Commerce (honours in Accounting) in addition to a professional Indian qualification for banking in finance. When asked why P8 decided to leave India and immigrate to Canada, he stated "I don't know, really." P8 continued to add that he simply saw an advertisement claiming that Canada was the best country to live in, and he thought "OK, best country to live in, and we are so unhappy here." Therefore, he claims that his choice to immigrate to Canada was formed without much thought, investigation, or research of Canada and its job prospects.

P8 assumed that there would be a job waiting for him, due to his education and work experience in India. However, P8 had a significantly difficult transition, particularly within the career domain. P8 therefore completed many courses within the Canadian Securities Institute program and also enrolled in Seneca College to pursue a post-graduate certificate.

Shortly after completing one of the CSI courses, P8 was hired at an investment firm, but states that he had to quit as he wasn't able to find clients due to his lack of connections within Canada. After enrolling in further courses, P8 was not successful in attaining a job of his choice. He is currently employed in a grocery store in customer service, where he helps customers bring groceries to their cars. He stated that he is planning on taking an additional course within a few months as an attempt to hopefully gain subsequent employment that is related to his area of interest.

Participant 9

Participant 9 (P9) is a 44-year-old male who emigrated from India in January 2002 when he was 34 years of age. P9 completed his Master's degree in Commerce with a major in Accounting. Before immigrating to Canada, he was a self-employed business owner. He began his own business within metal fabrication, and had an additional business where he sold garments to the Middle East. While he shares that he was completely satisfied with his businesses, he was seeking a better quality of life; thus, his motivation to immigrate to Canada was to acquire this higher quality of personal life.

P9 found the job-search process extremely challenging; while he secured many jobs, they were simply survival jobs and he found that his skills were being underutilized. Therefore, P9 made the decision to apply to MBA programs. After he wrote his GMATS, he was accepted to and subsequently enrolled in the MBA program. Following his completion of this degree, he acquired his first job within an MBA rotation program. Subsequently, P9 interviewed for several jobs and was able to secure one which was relevant to his background and education. Although P9 is currently looking for a new job (as he does not believe his current organization offers room for growth and development), he is very satisfied with all other aspects of his current job and career-life.

Participant 10

Participant 10 (P10) is a 42-year-old woman who emigrated from the Philippines when she was 35 years of age. She arrived in Canada with her husband and daughter in January 2005. P10's pre-Canada education consists of a Bachelor of Social Work, in addition to a Master's degree in Management. The degrees took 4 years and 2 years to complete, respectively. Before immigrating to Canada, P10 was employed as a Community Development Supervisor. While she states that she was not financially satisfied with this job, she deemed it as being very personally rewarding. Although P10 was very happy in her current job, she decided to move to Canada due to the current recession and uncertainty within her job. In addition, she recalls seeing many flyers indicating the need for social workers within Canada, and therefore thought it would offer her family a better life.

P10 describes the transition to Canada as being very difficult; she was simultaneously employed in 3 survival jobs for approximately 9 months. After ending this employment, she enrolled in an MSW bridging program. P10 was hired while she was still enrolled in the bridging program, which was terminating on the day of her interview. She was very happy within that particular position, and is currently starting a new internship which will last three months.

OPTIMISM OR PESSIMISM AMONG IMMIGRANT EXPERIENCES

Participants were identified as optimists (P2 P5, P6, P10, and P9), pessimists (P3, P8, and P4), or as neutralists (P1, and P7). This allowed for a clear comparison between individuals' experiences based on their levels of optimism and pessimism. The following two sections are titled: Optimists and Pessimists, respectively. These sections each feature summaries of participants' experiences as new and professional immigrants in Canada,

Life-Career Themes 49

with particular focus on their retraining program. Lastly, the following sections also consider how participants dealt with and managed challengers and barriers encountered throughout their overall experience.

Optimists

Five of the ten participants were identified as being optimists within the present study (P2, P5, P6, P10, and P9). In an effort to concretize participant themes and to reduce researcher bias and influence throughout the coding process, it was required that an optimistic attitude be defined. The present researcher defined an optimistic attitude as not being necessarily tied to anticipation of specific improvements and progress (Pew Research Centre, 1999), but as "the habit of thinking that good events are caused by stable, global, and internal factors, whereas bad events are caused by unstable, specific, and external factors" (Lee & Seligman, 1997, p.32). Furthermore, an optimistic individual tends to express significant hope for the future, despite current circumstances. As a general and overall guideline, nodes were classified as being optimistic when participant narratives were generally viewed as expressive, cheerful, and confident in their origin (Lee & Seligman, 1997), particularly when the aforementioned definition was not entirely applicable. Therefore, when participants portrayed particular habits of thinking that reflected this guideline, their associated narratives were coded as holding an optimistic attitude. Implications of an optimistic attitude and additional themes are presented within the discussion chapter.

OPTIMISM AMIDST CHALLENGES

It is well researched and thus a commonly-known problem that new immigrants face a myriad of barriers upon their transition to a new country, including language barriers, cross-cultural difficulties, communication difficulties, isolation and retraining or reaccreditation (Dean & Wilson, 2009; Jafari, 2010; Reitz, 2001). Therefore, a significant number of immigrants are overcome with stress, anxiety and depression, in addition to multiple mental health impacts (Jafari, 2010). However, a prominent theme that presented itself during the findings was one where optimists described maintaining optimistic attitudes throughout their challenging transition and overall immigration experience. Therefore, despite the fact that participants suffered from an overwhelming transition, many of them maintained a positive frame of mind throughout their hardships. This current section signifies this optimistic attitude in regard to various challenges that were encountered, including immigration, personal and cultural factors, overall transition, and their retraining experience.

P2 describes that although there were challenges that coincided with her family's decision to immigrate to Canada, they kept a positive attitude. When asked whether such challenges impacted her well-being, she stated:

> "Not really because we are very strong minded, so we adjust to things really fast. We have a very positive attitude; high esteem and always positive and confident about doing everything" (P2).

Interestingly, both P2 and P5 shared similar concerns given the current economical state, and how it may impact their future work-life in Canada. Below are P2 and P5's respective concerns, including their optimistic stance on this situation,

> "With all the shortcuts and things you hear about the economy, we're always concerned: what will the future hold for you? So we just hope for the best" (P2).

> "I'm a bit concerned about Ontario having a higher unemployment rate than it used to have; however, I strongly believe in Canada's natural resources' worth, I would say, and I am thinking seriously to go up north where chances are better" (P5).

The previous statement given by P5 illustrates a realistic recognition of the province's current financial and economical situation; however, it also illustrates his mentality to approach such uncontrollable circumstances with a positive and active approach.

Examples of an optimistic theme which arose specifically within the retraining or education experience are presented in the next section.

Optimism and Retraining/Education Experience

Retraining plays a key role in countries experiencing high levels of immigration (Gorbatova & Eaglstein, 1998). However, the experience of retraining in a similar field or reeducating oneself in a completely new realm can be particularly daunting. While existing studies (Gorbatova & Eaglstein, 1998; Lockhead, 2003) have focused on the challenges that arise within the immigration and retraining process, the present study revealed many positive attitudes throughout the retraining process. Examples of such optimistic attitudes within their retraining/education experience are outlined below from several participants.

P10 expressed being positively surprised by many aspects within her Canadian education experience. For instance, she stated:

> "There was a lot of positive realization when doing all this retraining, personally and professionally. I think it really helped me to become a better person, and it also more than molded my personality. It makes me more knowledgeable. There's just a lot of other positive impacts resulting to that" (P10).

P6, on the other hand, expected her education experience to be a pleasant one. She had the following to say about her education experience,

> "I expected it to be a great school. I didn't really know before starting school how the entire on campus recruitment worked, so that was a pleasant surprise. Obviously I pursued my MBA to get a job, but I wasn't really sure how it worked. The fact that it was quite structured and supportive was a pleasant surprise" (P6).

For many of the newcomers, their training program provided them with valuable skills and tools that only strengthened their sense of optimism about the training or education experience. P2, P5, P6, P9, and P10 described having similar experiences in this particular sense. P2 described how having increased knowledge provided her with a positive attitude,

"I felt better and more positive because I had more knowledge, and there was so many different courses. I got so much knowledge from this course. The professors were really very good and the material they gave out was good. So many resources; they had us refer to books or the internet. There is so much available; there is so much information on the internet" (P2).

In addition, P5 stated that he felt connected to the style of education in Canada, which positively impacted his studies,

"I was very happy to be involved in such a new approach. For me, it was a new approach, and I thought "this is the way it should be done: the North American way." I understand it is the same with the U.S. who also have a similar wide angle of looking at things. So for me, it was a great experience, very satisfying" (P5).

P6 stated that she found a tremendous amount of value in the education program and took advantage of additional opportunities within her schooling,

"I really valued the education itself. I think the quality of the education, the rigor of the program was great. I really enjoyed the social aspect of it because I really got involved with all of the possible extra curricula, and that was a good way to not only meet people, but also learn a lot more about the "Canadian" way, which was helpful" (P6).

P9 commented particularly on the learning experience within the retraining program, and shared how (in his opinion) it was a significantly more positive experience to that of what he received in his home country,

"The learning experience in Canada was really good. I'm totally happy that I went for it. The learning experience itself is far superior to whatever I had in India. Like I said, we never had class participation or anything like

Life-Career Themes

53

that (in India). It was the lecture as well as the discussion, so the learning from here was diverse and superior, because there are people from all over the world (in Canada)" (P9).

Within this context, P10 added that her education experience positively impacted her experience as a new worker in Canada,

"It helps a lot in the way I approach people, in the way I deliver information, and also because it is really required of me to be one step more knowledgeable" (P10).

Many of the newcomers mentioned that peer support played a role in maintaining and strengthening their optimistic and positive attitude throughout the retraining program. Given that many of the newcomers are in similar circumstances and have similar reasons for taking the retraining or a new education program, they found it useful and important to develop mentorships and friendships throughout their experience. P6 discussed how her mentorship aided her throughout this process,

"I found a bunch of friends, and I was really starved for that kind of interaction. Everyone was in the same boat; I loved it" (P6).

She further noted:

"My partner, who I do a lot of work with, she mentors me a lot and that changed it completely. That made me a ton happier and a lot more confident. Good things. Feeling that somebody cares about you as a person; that you're not a cog in the system" (P6).

P2 echoed the positive attitude and feelings that resulted from peer support,

"I was so excited to have this opportunity and I was so excited about attending, and then you meet new friends. Our group was really good; we used to do projects together. We weren't stressed because we would study, and we'd simply talk about other things and laugh it out. It really helped.

We were so happy, so the group really helped. It is such a good experience, so fulfilling" (P2).

"A theme that arose by two of the participants illustrated their optimistic attitude during their retraining experience. Their initial concern was that their age may aversely influence their overall experience and ability. P2 cited this initial apprehension, which was quickly deterred once she was well-immersed in the program, I felt that at my age, would I be able to cope? But I was doing so well, so I was happy about that. As challenges came, I could manage" (P2).

She reiterated this opinion again during the interview, stating,

"I was really proud of myself that at the age of fifty, I graduated. I was so happy about that. And it is because I'm here in Canada that I could do it" (P2).

P5, also an older participant, echoed this initial apprehension surrounding his education in Canada, yet held a similar positive attitude throughout this process,

"To be honest with you, in the first month I was a bit apprehensive for not getting high marks. I thought that being older than my colleagues, I may be at a disadvantage. But after the first marks came, it was really positive. I had a moral boost because I had high marks right from the very beginning" (P5).

Some participants discussed how they viewed the retraining/education experience as a positive opportunity and chance for growth despite it being very easy to view the situation with resentment and a sense of bitterness. P2 noted the following of her retraining perspective,

"The things I enjoyed most was I felt like I was really young and going to school. I don't think that I could get that opportunity anywhere else, but Canada gave me that opportunity "(P2).

When asked of main lessons that she learned from her retraining experience in Canada, she stated,

> "First of all, anything is possible if you want to do it. Opportunity is there; it's upon the individual if you want to take it. There's so much available here: so many courses, so many colleges. It's up to the individual" (P2).

P9 echoed feeling gracious for this chance for development and growth, stating,

> "I saw it totally as an opportunity because I knew it would open up doors. If you're being negative, then there's no going forward" (P9).

P5 also noted this perspective about his retraining experience,

> "I feel quite positive. I'm not ashamed of sitting next to a person who is the age of my son or daughter. I don't mind that. I don't feel resentful; very proud" (P5).

An additional comment noted by P6 was centered around the distinction between retraining and a new education. She described that this distinction could be a component for her overall positive experience. She stated,

> "In my case, it wasn't retraining. It was training on top of my previous training. It wasn't like I'm a pharmacist coming in and I need to redo everything just to do the same thing. It was clearly something new, and on top of what I already had. And that's probably why I feel so positive about it, because it was an entirely new experience" (P6).

Optimism increased post-retraining/education experience. Retraining and education programs offer a wealth of potentially influencing variables. For instance, there are many plausible variables and factors that can positively or negatively impact one's experience in such a program. While much of the present literature discusses hardships and barriers for new immigrants (Dean & Wilson, 2009; Jafari, 2010), the literature fails to recognize how such retraining or education programs positively impact immigrants' overall attitudes and subsequent experience. The positive outcome and associated optimistic attitude that increased as a result of further education and/or training was a common theme within the present study. The current section thus details optimists' various descriptions and narratives, which explore their positive attitudes subsequent to their training experience.

P5 found that his new Canadian education influenced his perspective, stating,

> "The Canadian approach of a wide angle of looking at things has changed me, I think. I'm now a better trainer, a better instructor, and a better teacher than I used to be: more patient, more accepting of other views, even views that can be in collision or in conflict with my own views. I'm now open to accept them" (P5).

While P5 seemed to have an optimistic attitude throughout this process, it was strengthened even more as a result of his additional education,

> "My education and getting familiar with the Canadian atmosphere had a great impact as a new Canadian. The Canadian circumstances have helped me a lot with self esteem and with being proud to be a Canadian" (P5).

The majority of the participants stated that the retraining or additional Canadian education led them to become more encouraged to pursue their desired career. This can be extrapolated as the additional education experience having positively influenced their general attitude towards their career. Regardless of the fact that some optimists initially felt resentful after being told they should gain Canadian education and experience, they maintained an optimistic attitude and later shared their overall positive experience that resulted from this additional education. Many participants stated that the retraining served as a positive experience wherein they were able to develop a new sense of passion for their career that they originally trained in (in their home country). Alternatively, some participants stated that they found a new passion in a different field than they were originally trained. Some further stated that this experience gave them the opportunity to try a new career in a field that had always been an area of interest for them, but that of which was different than the field of their original career. Optimist narratives that particularly describe some of these perspectives are outlined below.

Optimism and Outcome

Given that the present study deemed it meaningful to focus on immigrant optimism within their Canadian retraining/education process, it is important to recognize those participant experiences where there seems to be a link between such optimism and participant career outcome.

Once P6 made the decision to seek education in Canada, she had an increasingly overall positive experience. P6 shared some insight that occurred after having been immediately employed following graduation. She stated,

> "I know it's going to sound very motherhood and apple pie, but (one of the main lessons I learned from my retraining experience) is that hard work actually pays off. I came with absolutely no connections, and I was able to land a fantastic job. For me, it's a huge thing, if you work really hard you can get what you want in this environment. To contrast this, in Ukraine, it's a little different. There's a lot more nepotism and who you know. You give bribes to get a job, which is unheard of here, but it's a different reality" (P6).

When asked how she felt about her future career development prospects in Canada, she added,

> "I feel positive, because I know that I will have options, even if I don't stay with my current company and current career, I'll be able to transition into something else. I feel like I'll have options if I choose to leave" (P6).

Like P6, P9 was also hired at a company directly from school. He describes some of the positive elements of the relationship between his retraining experience and his outcome in securing a career:

"I kept in touch with the HR person; this was in October and either January or February she called me and she said, "Look, these aren't full-time positions; they're contract positions just for the year." I said, "I'll take it." So I went for the interview; she gave me this thing, I researched on that topic and went in. Two or three days later I went in to the manager and he was completely blown away by the research I had done. In fact, I had gone and identified 3 of the 4 companies that should be doing this job, and it was bang on and he was totally impressed, and I was instantly hired" (P9).

When speaking about his current job, he added,

"I love it here. You need 3 things in a job: you need job satisfaction; there should be good money; and there should be growth prospects. I don't see growth prospects in this company, which is why I'm looking elsewhere, but I love everything else about it. Job satisfaction-wise, I'm totally there" (P9).

P5 also spoke of high job satisfaction and correspondingly, an optimistic attitude,

"Now, being a teaching assistant in a university, I would say I enjoy a very high level of job satisfaction. I'm happy teaching, holding and leading seminars, teaching things that I did and that I'm quite familiar with. It's very good" (P5).

When asked how useful his additional Canadian education had been, he added,

"Very useful, because once I had the MA degree, I could easily get jobs as a teaching assistant. I didn't have to confine myself to a particular university. I could have easily got a job at (several) universities" (P5).

Life-Career Themes

59

Identification of attitude as important. Many of the participants recognized their attitude as playing a significant role within their overall experience. More particularly, optimists identified their attitude as playing an integral role in their experience and career development. When P9 was asked about any career-related lessons that he has learned throughout this process, he shared some perspective that again, identifies attitude as being significant to one's career growth and development:

> "I would say that perception over here is everything, right? That's one thing that I've learned, that how people perceive you...very often your growth depends on that. Also, I saw this retraining as an opportunity because I knew it would open up doors. If you're being negative, then there's no going forward" (P9).

P5, who has expressed only positive views of his experience in Canada, shares some perspectives that may have been integral in maintaining his optimistic attitude and his willingness to adapt to external and uncontrollable circumstance. He stated:

> "My understanding is that a newcomer needs to adapt. Canada doesn't change for us. We have to change ourselves and our attitudes to suit Canada. So one has to be ready as a newcomer to adapt to the new environment to the best of their ability" (P5).

P2 also stated that her high self-esteem and optimistic outlook had a significant influence on her ability to be prepared for various unforeseen circumstances. When asked how she coped with difficulties, she stated:

> "High self-esteem and constantly being positive and confident about doing everything makes a big difference. Because of this, I can adjust to difficulties very fast" (P2).

Optimism and the Role of Choice and Control on Career Development

The present study found a prominent relationship between optimists and their belief of control over the majority of events and experiences. For instance, optimists believed that their conscious choice and active control played an integral role in their career development experience, rather than the role of chance. Possible support and rationale for this apparent link will be further elaborated on within the discussion section. The excerpts below provide meaning for the apparent relationship between optimists and the belief of control over circumstances and experiences in Canada.

The following narratives are taken from participants who were determined by the present researcher as being optimistic about their career-life experience in Canada; particularly regarding their retraining/education experiences. When asked about the role of choice in her life and career in Canada, P6 acknowledges that luck may have played a role, but dictates that active engagement and choice were the primary factors that are responsible for her current situation. P6 responded in the following manner:

> "Considering everything so far, it is definitely choice that played a role. The fact that I've been typically quite lucky in my life when the right people come along and nudge you and give you good advice; that was always very important. But I felt like I made a decision, so it wasn't chance- it was a choice to go to school. It was a choice to take courses that I did, and apply for jobs that I did" (P6).

P9 noted a similar perspective in that he recognized chance as playing a role in his life, but describes that he must be responsible and realize that he has to take the reins in his life:

> "Oh, chance plays a role. In anybody's life, you've got to be in the right place at the right time. But that doesn't mean that you wait for things to happen; you have to make things happen as well, so it's a mix of both. There are things that you help yourself, but God helps sometimes" (P9).

P5 credits the role of choice in his life as being a critical component in his career-life experience in Canada:

> "I had a lot of choice here in Canada. Before immigrating to Canada, my choices were narrow, limited. Here in Canada, I feel that I have more choices; it's more open. There are events that influence the way you take decisions. For example, the event of my son getting accepted in a particular university; therefore, driving me to attend this university rather than other institutions within this province. Yes, events were influential, but not very much. I still had plenty of choice- choice is a big factor" (P5).

PESSIMISTS

Three of the ten participants were identified as being pessimists within the present study (P3, P8, and P4). The present researcher defined the presence of a pessimistic attitude when individuals reported feeling victimized by events or powerless to do anything about them (Neimark, 1987). Furthermore, pessimistic individuals typically have very little hope for their future, believe that they have no control over circumstances or external events, and are more likely to report experiencing depressive symptoms and increased stress (Lee & Seligman, 1997; Neimark, 1987). The experience of new immigrants is undoubtedly a difficult one and it is thus understandable that new immigrants will experience periods of doubt. However, excerpts from the following individuals portray a chronic characterization of hopelessness, belief in a lack of control, and an overall negative attitude regarding their experiences. Therefore, the aforementioned definitions and guidelines were used as a means of identifying pessimistic participants within the present study. Their attitudes and experiences are detailed within various transition and career development experiences in Canada.

Pessimism throughout Challenges and Retraining Experiences

It was previously asserted in one of the themes that many of the participants maintained their optimistic attitude amidst various challenges as new and professional immigrants. This section, however, recognizes participant narratives whose pessimism increased as a result of the barriers they were confronted with in their new country. This pessimistic and hopeless attitude seemed to largely influence their overall experience and transition in Canada, in addition to their retraining/education and corresponding career outcome.

P7 was one of the few participants who did not have a positive retraining experience. He discussed how this experience did not live up to his expectations:

"The retraining experience actually discouraged me, until I did extra courses. Not that I was going to do it, but that sort of sapped all of my confidence and self-esteem. There was no (self-esteem) when I graduated. Maybe they do that by design" (P7).

P3 described feeling thwarted and inhibited throughout the majority of his experience in Canada. Particularly, his career search proved to be very exasperating:

"I feel that I'm fighting every day. I'm not enjoying life, I'm fighting. This, actually, is what presses on myself. Not self-esteem, but inside of myself. I'm very, very, very much exhausted. It makes an impact for myself. I try to encourage myself, but if you ask me if I enjoy life? No; I can be smiling, I can be joking, I can be whatever, but I'm not enjoying it because I need to pay bills each month. I have debt, interest rate, I have kids. It is not getting better" (P3).

A few of the participants grew very frustrated after applying to several jobs and not receiving any responses or positive outcomes. This lack of positive response seemed to have a significant impact on participants' self-esteem, mental health, and overall attitude.

Life-Career Themes 63

P7 stated that the transition experience produced mental and emotional exhaustion and disappointment throughout his job search:

> "When I initially came here, it was very difficult, because I couldn't get work for about a year and a half. I mean, nothing serious; it was all temporary jobs and I was very depressed for about a year and a half because I couldn't find work. I figured I would come here, people would see that I lived in an affluent section of town and that I come from a background of the United States, but it didn't really matter. You go to interview after interview, you don't get the job, or you don't even get calls. Just keep working; keep working towards something is what I did. I was depressed; my self-esteem was low, and I had no hope" (P7).

P4 was unemployed for 3 years after immigrating to Canada, as he was not permitted to have a Canadian visa. Being unable to work for three years was quite discouraging for P4:

> "It was very disappointing; it was a very dark bit of my life. I think that does impact immigrants in how they perceive Canada as a new home. It could just be a very personal reason, but if I was allowed to work and study immediately, maybe I would be more accepting in Canada as a new home" (P4).

P4 added that despite having the retraining, he remains unsettled within his career:

> "It's disappointing that I still don't feel happy in my career, because once you lose sometime, it just kind of falls into a pattern and affects you, and then your life falls into negativity; it creeps in. There's also something to do with your personality and adjustment and all of that, too. However, I forced myself in getting the Canadian label which ultimately ended up in nothing. It's kind of negatively impacted my career goals and everything. I mean, my career progress, I would say" (P4).

There was some contradiction in terms of P4's perspectives on financial support for retraining. For instance, despite P4 previously acknowledging that financial support was not needed for his retraining experience, he expressed negative feelings and judgments about not receiving retraining funding. This statement provides support that P4's pessimistic attitude is influencing many of his perspectives and his general Canadian experience:

"I self-financed myself for each and every course. I think that was a disappointment, as well. Like the bank I'm working for, even there, they won't pay me for anything. I have to get the certification to do this job, the career I want, and even you do not pay for that" (P4).

P4 described a negative outlook at individuals who were employed in jobs, which he felt he was more deserving of. He described some of this resentment below, where he stated:

"I would go to the banks; I would speak to people who work there, and I know as a matter of fact that I know more than them. But still, I can't find a job. I am willing to do a job for a lesser salary, but I think networking is a big thing. You have to have a network, and how can immigrants have a network?" (P4)

When asked about his feelings and attitude following his retraining experience, P4 stated:

"No one had this much certification that I have. Some of them were just high school people, but I realize they have been there for 5-6 years. Some of them are in the manager position, and they don't know the basics, so that is a big disappointment" (P4).

P8 was another individual who expressed deep discouragement and negativity regarding many aspects of his experience in Canada. The following excerpts from his interview reflect his pessimistic attitude and current perspective of having given up:

"When I came here, I used to believe that because of my experience, I'll get a job for sure. But now I know that's not going to happen. So, any job which I can do, with the level of my health and physical capacity allows

Life-Career Themes

65

me to, that is good. So every day, I'm changing my level of expectation to one that is more real; it just won't happen for me" (P8).

In the following statement, he expressed an abysmal attitude surrounding his outlook, where he stated:

"They are always recruiting people for their classes, like ESL classes, resume-writing classes, how to keep your positive mental attitude. I don't know how many kinds of classes, but they didn't help me. Now it is that I don't go to those centers because I know I'm not going anywhere" (P8).

On a similar note, he stated the following quote and its applicability to his current circumstance:

"You don't have any rights to the fruits of your work; you have only the right to work. So now, I believe in those words so deeply. I'm just doing my work without expecting anything. I have no expectation" (P8).

When discussing his future, P8 stated:

"There is no point in leaving this job and going to another job unless they fire me or they lay me off. I'm not going to get anything better, so why should I leave this and try to find another? It's so difficult now. I'm not blaming anybody, but what I feel is I'm done here; it's too much. At this point in time, I don't expect anything. Unless it really comes, I cannot believe it. I have no further hope" (P8).

Lastly, when P8 was asked what his most important career-related lessons learned were, he answered:

"Don't expect the things you are looking for. Accept what you get. This is my real life experience: whatever I was looking for, I never got it. So, I learned how to accept whatever I got. I have no option" (P8).

Identification of Attitude as Important

The previous section identified optimists who stated that their optimistic attitude played an important role in their career development and their overall experience. However, the present study also found that two of the three pessimists (P3 and P4) identified their attitudes as important components within their career development experience in Canada. For instance, pessimists expressed the need to change their attitudes from a negative to a positive one, to allow for an increased chance of positive events to occur. In particular, pessimistic participants asserted the need to re-evaluate and subsequently change their attitude to being more positive.

P3 was identified as a pessimistic participant who was disappointed with his experience and transition to Canada. He expressed that despite having a negative experience in Canada, he was still able to identify that his attitude had a great deal to do with his experience in Canada. He stated the following about his insights regarding attitude:

> "If you're here, you have 2 choices, either to fight or just go home. It has a lot to do with attitude. What I like very much, even with negative experience, emotions, and even stress, what I like in Canada very much, at least compared to my country, is that you can always go and find a job that can make a more or less decent living income for yourself. I have a negative attitude now, but I will try to encourage myself, I will try to find out some positives. Once you start to think negatively, you're done" (P3).

He also asserted that his attitude has to be in the right place in order for him to learn successfully within the retraining program. More particularly, he stated:

> "In my case, I did not have stress from learning, because in order to learn successfully and fast and get good results on the exam, you need to be positive, even if you hate what you study. In order to put something in my brain, some information, I need to assimilate it, and I can only do that when I'm positive. I can say "it's a waste of my time," but bottom line, it doesn't matter what I think, it should be done. That's why I need to concentrate on the positive. I am hoping my confidence will open more doors for me in the future" (P3).

Life-Career Themes   67

P4 was also identified as a pessimistic participant who was not content with his circumstances since immigrating to Canada. The following excerpts provide P4's realization that one's perspective and explanatory style has an impact on his/her outcomes and future. He noted the following in regards to this recognition:

> "You have to change your ways, right? I realize that if I don't change my ways, then I'll get only frustrated. And that frustration and negativity will make me suffer even more. That's something that I learned about myself. I realized that I have to bury all the negativity and frustration that I've built up in all these years; that I'm not going to get anywhere being like this" (P4).

P4 later expressed some of the resentment and bitterness that had built up since immigrating to Canada after not acquiring career success or happiness. However, he seems to connect this with his current circumstance of being pessimistic and how this attitude and resentment is only negatively impacting him, and possible hindering his future prospects. He stated:

> "I do have a lot of bitterness, and right now I need to get rid of the bitterness. That's the major factor because positivity is very important in life, right? If you're positive, you will get opportunities, you will be recognized and you will use it. No matter how skilled you are...like they say, you get fired for your skills or get fired for behaviour or attitude. So, attitude and positivity is very important. I would say that I lost opportunities for having a negative attitude. So right now, my focus is to gain that positivity that I had before immigrating" (P4).

When P4 was asked about the main lessons that he learned throughout his immigration and transition process, he once again brought the importance of attitude into his answer. P4 stated:

> "One word: attitude. No matter how many setbacks or frustrations or disappointments you had, you cannot push it on the opportunities you already have or what you're getting. So you have to feel gratitude for what you're getting. This is something that I'm trying to think. Okay, maybe my

work-life is not successful in Canada, but look how beautiful this country is. Look at all of the beautiful people you get to see here. Just trying to be more positive. Canada is a great country; it's good for immigrants, and it has a lot of opportunities if our attitude is right" (P4).

Pessimists and the Role of Chance on Career Development

The previous section portrayed an apparent link between optimistic participants and their belief of choice and control over their experiences. Alternatively, pessimistic participants in the present study believed that chance played a significant role in the result of their life-career experiences and events. The following narratives dictate pessimists' attitudes surrounding these roles of choice and chance within their experiences and in their ultimate outcomes.

P3 focused his perspective on the more significant role that chance has played in his life:

"Some events, unfortunately, I cannot control, and I asked myself why it happened with myself. Some people in my life, unfortunately, not even did they not help me, or even tried to make a lot of problems for me in my career, personal life, and so on. I ask myself "I don't understand, you see I'm an immigrant, I'm trying hard- why are you giving me problems?" I did not understand" (P3).

Moreover, P4 has an interesting perspective in terms of the choice/chance role in his life. More particularly, his perspective seems to consist of a self-serving bias. That is, he appears to be attributing his successes to internal factors and his failure to situational factors that are beyond his control. When asked about the role of choice and chance in his life, he stated the following,

"It starts with a choice; when it doesn't work out, it becomes chance. It was my choice to leave India. I couldn't have foreseen the situations I would meet in the U.S., like the U.S. economy going south, and that as a foreign student, I would have difficulty finding a job. I would have no financial support" (P4).

Lastly, P8 provides his view on the role of choice and chance in his life. It is apparent within the following excerpt that P8 has very little hope, and believes he has very little, or no control of his future:

"It is all because of chance events. Everybody's saying the same thing...wherever they've taken me, I'm going. I really have no option at this time. Everything is out of my control; I have no option, so I don't know whether I will be able to complete the designation or not. If everything happens in the way I planned for, then I look for an accounting job; But nothing is sure; I cannot predict" (P8).

SELF-EFFICACY

The following section will focus on participants' self-efficacy, or efficacy beliefs. That is, it includes themes that were identified as an individual's portrayal of self-efficacy throughout various circumstances of their immigration and transition. For the purpose of this research, we chose to define self-efficacy as the individuals' perceptions about their own abilities to successfully perform a task (Bandura, 1986). Therefore, when a narrative corresponded with this definition, it was categorized into an appropriate self-efficacy theme. The following themes explore participant narratives citing their efficacy beliefs before the training/education program, and efficacy beliefs during and after the training/education program.

Self-Efficacy before Retraining/Education Program

Because many of the participants had a positive experience with education and school in their home country, their self-efficacy beliefs were quite high before beginning the training/education program in Canada. The majority of narratives within this section were formulated as responses to the following question: "Thinking about your pre-Canada skills and abilities, how did you think you would perform in the retraining program?"

P6 was among one of the participants who had a positive education experience in her home country, and thus used this experience as a relative predictor for her performance in Canada. Despite the fact that she was pursuing education in a new field, she had high self-efficacy for her performance and abilities. She noted the following about her efficacy beliefs in relation to her Canadian experience:

> "Maybe it will sound arrogant, but I knew I would do well when I'm in school. I generally tend to do well at school, so I wasn't really worried" (P6).

P9 was another participant who had to develop new skills and knowledge in Canada, as he planned on pursuing education within a new field. Nonetheless, his efficacy beliefs remained heightened:

> "I had confidence; I don't think it had anything to do with my skills in India because that was such a general thing. I knew my experience from India would be helpful, but I didn't have any of the skills that are required for business school; I had to develop them here. But I had general business knowledge which includes finance, marketing, accounting, but not as much for HR. (However), I had those core business strategies, I had an understanding of it; so that knowledge is transferable to any field, which definitely helped me" (P9).

P3 specifically did retraining within the same field and therefore did not have many difficulties when thinking about how he would perform in the retraining program. He had a high sense of efficacy when reflecting back to his skills and abilities that were developed from his host country:

> "I was confident that I would perform well. I didn't have any problems with English as a language, and secondly, because of particular definitions (in my field). If you ask me what is a mutual fund, I can explain it. I won't

ask you what it is. I used to know financial definitions and what they mean and so on. Basically, it was only necessary to learn how it works, what it's for, and that's it" (P3).

P1 shared P3's confidence and efficacy beliefs, as he already felt quite confident with his existing knowledge in his given domain:

"I felt pretty comfortable (about finding work in my profession), because I'm very experienced in my field" (P1).

The nature of P2's retraining experience was building onto her existing knowledge. Therefore, her training program consisted of both old and new information. She expressed feeling very positive and having high efficacy beliefs for her program, as it was a great opportunity to use existing skills and abilities, but would also serve as a significant learning experience:

"I was already prepared for all of the retraining here because every job I did there and all of those years I worked in Kenya, my skills were already built up. I was using a typewriter so my speed was good; I was using computers; and all of the administrative duties, like customer service on the phone, in person, all of those were developed and I applied all of my knowledge here. I had so much confidence for the (training) program. I was okay making a compromise for my retraining choice because I was really confident that I wanted to do something, and because I was so confident with the course work" (P2).

Interestingly, P10 did not have high efficacy for her retraining program, despite the fact that she would be training within the same field. For this participant, her efficacy regarding her language and communication skills influenced her efficacy for her overall performance:

"I didn't think I would be able to do it. Even talking to people, it's so difficult. The more that you focus, the more that you'll have mispronunciations. It's so difficult when I talk to people the first time; it's really challenging. I don't know what I'm talking about" (P10).

Self-Efficacy during and Following the Retraining/Education Program

While one's efficacy beliefs about their performance within and subsequent to the retraining program were brought into the interview at various times, several questions served as prompts to have participants reflect on their efficacy and confidence levels during and after the program.

While P10's efficacy and confidence levels were very low before she began the training program, she noted having increased efficacy beliefs for her abilities during the program:

"Now that I am in my MSW program, I would consider that I do have a lot of experiences. During discussion, I can contribute more because my ideas were something that they didn't experience here. So, maybe the uniqueness of my experience there is good in a way to deepen the understanding of the concept or the theories" (P10).

Interestingly, P10's efficacy beliefs increased even more when she referred to her confidence in her skills and abilities following her training program. She shares this increased efficacy and elaborates on some particular skills that were developed through her training program in Canada. Her new sense of confidence and pride is both implicit and explicit within her narrative. P10 stated:

"My skills were really polished. I really had a lot of terminologies that I didn't use before; I didn't even understand. Also the way you do things-let's say confidentiality. We don't have so much confidentiality in the Philippines. Even the concept of that is different from here. So that alone, the way you touch things like that in a very practical way. Just by observing normal people in your day to day (functioning); I get to learn that and embrace that, and do that as a way of life" (P10).

Life-Career Themes 73

P6 described gaining a deep enjoyment from her education experience which evolved into increased confidence and efficacy for her overall abilities:

"I think this competitive aspect really came out. People dreaded all of these interviews, competition and all of that; I thrived on that. For me, having very specific feedback and reinforcement about doing well; that keeps me going. I knew I was competitive, but it was never that vividly in my face" (P6).

In focusing on P9's skills and abilities after the training program, he noted that his efficacy beliefs improved significantly:

"I would say my (skills and abilities) improved considerably in every aspect, including communication and of course the financial skills; the knowledge that you have and how to present yourself and talk to people. Completely, the training has changed you" (P9).

P9 adds:

"(The training program) definitely improves your self-esteem. People look at you differently because you have a Canadian degree from one of the best schools in Canada, so doors open up. They think you're acceptable, and they look at you and you feel you're capable; you're capable to do it. That's the biggest difference" (P9).

P6 also discussed particular skills that her education program provided her with and strengthened, ultimately giving her the confidence to deal with novel situations following her education:

"I was always very interested in diversity and learning new things and I get bored easily doing the same thing. This education and this career played up very strongly to that. I think that it helped me deal much better with its ambiguity. I'm much better at facing an ambiguous situation rather than something predictable" (P6).

Additionally, P5 expressed that although he had an optimistic attitude and hoped he would perform well within his Canadian education, the new knowledge increased his confidence in his abilities much more. He simply stated:

> "I feel a lot better about my skills since my new education. I'm quite confident that I understand now, at this moment, environmental policies very well. My education has opened better chances for me as a new worker in Canada" (P5).

P10 was in a unique circumstance, as this research interview took place on the last day of her position. She was scheduled to be starting a new position very soon. P10's education provided her with increased self-efficacy within a practical setting. She had the following to say about her current position and career outcome:

> "I feel so happy that I'm able to connect to people, and I feel so accomplished that I'm able to do what I was able to do in the organization that wasn't done by anyone before, and I was acknowledged for that. That is where the realization comes in: Oh, I am able to do it, and I've made a lot of difference to people" (P10).

Chapter 5

CAREER OPTIMISM AND SELF-EFFICACY

Findings presented in the proceeding chapter are reviewed and discussed within the present chapter. The results emphasized immigrant levels of optimism and pessimism, and compared experiences and outcomes among optimists and pessimists. In addition, the results examined immigrant levels of self-efficacy before, during, and following participants' retraining programs. This final chapter will review and discuss the findings by exploring new and professional immigrants within the following areas: 1) Optimists' career development experiences, 2) Pessimists' career development experiences, 3) Differences among optimists' and pessimists' career development experiences, and 4) The influence of individual self-efficacy among immigrants' career development experience. Each of these sections are further categorized to include appropriate and relevant findings. The implications of the study's findings for practice are also addressed. Lastly, limitations of the present study are considered, in addition to directions and recommendations for future researchers interested in exploring this area.

OPTIMISTS' CAREER DEVELOPMENT EXPERIENCES

While positive psychology (Seligman, 1991) is one of the newer realms of psychology, it has made astounding findings and has portrayed strong relationships across many variables. In particular, optimists tend to experience less stress (Scott, 2011), have superior health (Peterson, 2000), live longer (Peterson et al., 1988), have greater achievement regardless of actual skills (Seligman, 1995), in addition to experiencing many more favourable outcomes. The relationship between optimism and career development has also been well-documented in recent research. For instance, research has portrayed links between optimists and high levels of career planning and exploration, confidence regarding career decisions, and high levels of career-related goals (Creed et al, 2002). In this realm, optimism has also been related to higher self-esteem (Patton et al., 2002), self-efficacy and career-adaptability (Rottinghaus, Day, & Borgen, 2005), career satisfaction (Lounsbury, Park, Sundstorm, Williamson, & Pemberton, 2004), and career success (Lau & Shaffer, 1999). Lastly, it has recently been shown that optimists are able to secure jobs more easily and with less effort than their non-optimistic counterparts, and were more likely to be promoted 2 years after graduation (Kaniel et. al, 2010). Given these strong relationships in the context of optimism and career development, the present research focused on optimism as a key tenet within the immigrant retraining and career development process.

Overall, this study suggests that those individuals who possess a more optimistic outlook tend to experience what is primarily a more positive retraining and career development process. Moreover, the findings suggest that there appears to be a link between professional immigrants' levels of optimism and many favourable outcomes within their retraining and overall career development experience. Many of these findings provide empirical support that optimists were better able to manage and positively experience unforeseen challenges and barriers (Lamb, 2009; Riolli et al., 2004; Scott, 2011), in addition to positively experiencing their retraining experiences and career outcomes (Kaniel & Massey, 2010; Lau & Shaffer, 1999; Lounsbury et al., 2004). Furthermore, optimists in the present study identified their attitudes as playing integral roles in their career development experience, and believed that they had greater control over their lives and career experiences.

Career Optimism and Self-Efficacy 77

Optimism amidst Challenges

Encountering challenges such as cultural barriers and under/unemployment as new immigrants in Canada is extremely common, and many new immigrants consequently experience high levels of stress and negative health impacts (Dean & Wilson, 2009; Jafari, 2010). However, the present findings explored optimists' perspectives and experiences with these common challenges, and found that they were better able to cope with and overcome hardships within their career development experience. This was demonstrated by participants' ability to view their hardships as experiences that were surmountable and as an opportunity in which they could learn. While there is no known literature exploring the relationship between immigrant optimists' and their ability to handle transitional challenges, these findings are consistent with positive psychology literature. For example, positive psychology literature has found that optimists tend to perceive unforeseen hardships as learning experiences as opposed to difficult challenges, or additional stressors in which they are not able to cope (Scott, 2011). Additionally, optimists have portrayed better internal strength and ability to cope with stressors and hardships than their pessimistic peers (Lamb, 2009; Riolli et al., 2004). Therefore, what are typically seen as challenging experiences to pessimists tend to induce hope for tomorrow in optimistic individuals (Lamb, 2009). This research was congruent with the present study's findings; optimists' attitudes and perspectives throughout their hardships and challenges were admirable, resilient, and hopeful, where one optimistic participant stated "we just hope for the best" (P2).

The present study's findings on optimists and challenges also resemble the career development literature on career resilience. In particular, career resilience is typically demonstrated by individuals' ability to cope with daily hardships and stressors that they encounter (Amundson et al., 2004). Career resilience has also been characterized by the individual's ability to maintain an optimistic, positive and focused attitude, a portrayal of flexibility, as well as organization and proactive measures taken by the individual (Hagevik, 1998). Therefore, it is suggested that resilient and optimistic individuals have similar experiences, perspectives, and means of coping with career development hardships (Amundson et al., 2004). While participants in the present study were not explicitly questioned about their resilience within their Canadian experience, many of their optimistic tendencies and perspectives embodied resiliency characteristics.

There are many potential reasons why optimists are able to effectively handle challenges and barriers. In addition to their attitude as playing a foundational role in overcoming challenges, this study's findings emphasized the importance of peer support. Optimists expressed feelings of strength and support generated from close friendships with peers who were struggling with similar concerns and stressors. While this theme is well-researched within the career development literature (Berry, 1997; Clement, Noels, & Deneault, 2001; Neto, 1995; Ward, Bochner, & Furnham, 2001), its importance for the well-being of new and professional immigrants is integral. Peer and social support have been shown to play significant roles in improving the adjustment difficulties among immigrants (Ward et al., 2001); mainly, peer support provides immigrants with emotional and informational support (Berry, 1997; Neto, 1995), in addition to relating on matters such as experiencing discrimination, stress, and incongruities among aspects of one's identity (Clement et al., 2001). In addition to serving as this emotional support for participants, they also described that having this peer and social support provided them with a necessary outlet that they would not otherwise have. For example, participants were able to better cope with stressors of their transition process and retraining program given the strong peer and social support that they had. These supports were not only effective as a means of coping and support throughout their programs, but many participants recalled maintaining friendships with such individuals, as they had such a profound impact on one another's lives. Furthermore, some participants have identified some of their supports as being informal mentors and still rely on them throughout their various stressors, circumstances, and careers.

Optimists' Retraining Experience and Career Outcomes

In this study, it was found that optimistic individuals appeared to have a more pleasurable training experience, and expressed positive attitudes pertaining to the retraining programs. There are many factors and perspectives that may have contributed to this pleasurable experience for optimists, when compared to their pessimistic counterparts. For example, the findings suggested that optimists were more likely to see the retraining program as a positive opportunity for growth, as opposed to bearing feelings of anger and resentment. In addition, many optimists used their retraining opportunity as a chance to explore an area of interest and gain new knowledge, as opposed to relearning material in their originally trained career.

Optimists also experienced satisfaction with their current personal and professional life. This was demonstrated by participants' narratives where they expressed a state of satisfaction and fulfillment with their careers and lives, in addition to their overall career development experience in Canada. These findings are similar with research that has been conducted in non-immigrant populations. For instance, researchers found that even when optimists and pessimists have similar skills, optimists spent less effort searching for a job, were offered jobs more quickly, were even more likely to be promoted, and had higher levels of career satisfaction (Kaniel & Massey, 2010). Finally, the present study suggested that optimists experience high levels of satisfaction within their retraining programs and overall career outcomes (Kaniel & Massey, 2010; Lyubomirsky, 2001), and portrayed that this relationship is present among the immigrant population.

PESSIMISTS' CAREER DEVELOPMENT EXPERIENCES

Pessimists, Challenges, and Their Retraining Experience

In the preceding section, it was discussed that optimists were better able to persevere throughout challenges within their overall career development and retraining experience. Alternatively, pessimists in the present study expressed increased difficulties in persevering throughout their hardships. For instance, one participant (P4) had difficulty attaining a visa and therefore could not work for a significant period of time. This hardship had a snowball effect on various aspects of P4's life, as a negative attitude was a prominent theme in many of his narratives. In addition, P8's pessimism was explicit throughout his hopeless stance. He frequently stated that he had no control, hope, that nothing would ever improve, and that he was going no where (P8). These examples of hopelessness and overwhelming pessimism are consistent with existing literature (Amundson et al., 2004; Riolli et al., 2004). Existing literature suggests that pessimists struggle in the face of environmental stressors, have difficulty overcoming their problems through appraisal and direct coping, and tend to internalize their barriers (Riolli et al., 2004). This is also present within the present study, where some pessimists' portrayed inhibited attitudes and took a passive rather than active career development stance (Amundson et al., 2004). The present study's narratives display this link between pessimists and an increased difficulty overcoming challenges, which align with the existing literature. Overall, pessimists' abilities to see positive opportunities or to characterize signs of resiliency were minimal within the present study.

The findings also suggested that pessimists were less likely to see their retraining programs and educational experiences as a positive opportunity for growth. Instead, many of the pessimists entered their retraining experience with bitterness and resentment. In addition, they were more likely to complain about various factors regarding the retraining experience, such as financial aspects (P4, P7) and a lack of a positive learning experience (P7). In particular, three participants stated that they believed the retraining experiences were discouraging, that their classes did not offer anything, and that the experiences actually harmed their career development (P4, P7, P8).

Differences among Optimists' and Pessimists' Experiences

As previously mentioned, optimists in the present study appeared to have overall more favourable outcomes and a more successful career development experience than pessimistic immigrants. Many of the pessimist participants believed that they were stuck, had little control for their future, and developed negative frameworks for how the world ran, particularly in terms of their career development. Pessimists' struggles and origin of their developed attitudes appear understandable, given their hardships and arduous career development experience in Canada. However, there is a significant difference when pessimists' narratives are compared to narratives from their optimistic counterparts. In particular, both optimists and pessimists endure a similar Canadian process: they encounter unexpected hardships and barriers, must undergo retraining or pursue further education, and must then seek a job within their area of expertise. Despite the similarities in this process after arriving in Canada, their attitude and overall cognitive style appears to be a key tenet that signifies the nature of their overall experience, how they handle their setbacks, and subsequent career development action. Moreover, optimists' characterized setbacks and hardships as being expected difficulties given that they were in a new country. Moreover, optimists expressed more understanding that barriers were likely to occur. In addition, they treated such hardships as learning experiences, and maintained their positive perspective on their future career development, as opposed to bearing resentment. This is consistent with literature in support of optimists who are resilient amidst hardships (Amundson et al., 2004; Hagevik, 1998). Overall, it was found that immigrant optimists tend to make the most of all experiences, including their hardships, and are quite flexible in terms of necessary career development changes (Lamb, 2009). This finding suggests a connection between an open minded attitude and career development, which may provide support for Chen's (2004) positive compromise framework. Chen's (2004) positive compromise framework suggests that an open mind serves as the foundation for imagination, creativity, and flexibility, which is of critical importance in adopting change and creating optimal circumstances to allow for a positive compromise (Chen, 2004).

Lastly, an interesting finding appeared when comparing optimists and pessimists, wherein many of the participants credited their attitude as playing an integral role in their overall experience and outcome. Although pessimists' attitudes were relatively discouraged, they recognized the negative influence that their attitude was having on their career satisfaction and overall career development experience. Pessimists expressed the need to take appropriate action to change their attitudes. Overall, this finding presumably speaks to the power of both optimistic and pessimistic attitudes throughout various career development experiences.

The Influence of Control or Chance among Optimists and Pessimists

As outlined in the preceding findings chapter, optimists and pessimists differed in terms of how much control they believed they possessed over particular circumstances and their career development experience as a whole. Participants were asked to what degree of control they believed they carried within their Canadian career experience, or if they believed chance played the more significant role in dictating their current set of circumstances.

While most optimists and pessimists recognized both chance and control as likely playing some role within their lives, the findings were staggering in terms of one's perception of chance and control. More particularly, participants who were identified as optimists stated that they had exhibited a significant amount of control over their career development and overall experience thus far in Canada. The link between optimism and perceived control over aspects of one's life has been consistently portrayed within positive psychology research (Fontaine, Manstead, & Wagner, 2006; Mishel, Hostetter, King, & Graham, 1984). Thus, the present finding suggests that this optimism-control link is also present within the professional immigrant population. Interestingly, pessimists were extremely adamant of the fact that chance played a primary role within their experience. Moreover, many pessimists expressed that they were hopeless, that there was nothing they could do, and that everything was out of their control. This latter description is consistent with Seligman's (1972) learned helplessness, where it is posited that when faced with events where one believes he or she has little or no control, one can feel debilitated. This debilitation can lead to learned helplessness, which can ultimately result in a state of depression (Seligman, 1972).

The links between optimism and control and pessimism and chance hold interesting implications for the professional immigrant population. Particularly, the findings suggest that when presented with chance opportunities, optimists are better able to apply a sense of control and capitalize on such opportunities (Chen, 2005; Cochran, 1990, 1997). Alternatively, it is plausible that their pessimistic counterparts, who became more easily discouraged by external events, lacked the ability or perspective necessary to act on the chance opportunities. By not taking action, pessimists likely became increasingly discouraged at the apparent lack of career development opportunities that were presented.

It was apparent within participant narratives that optimists, indeed, treated unforeseen circumstances as meaningful as opposed to meaningless. This was further characterized by their ability to recognize chance opportunities and to apply energy to the potential impact such opportunities may have on their career development experience. Altogether, this finding implies the importance that new and professional immigrants should place on the potential that lies within chance opportunities. For example, if professional immigrants simply believe that they have no control over particular career aspects, they will likely remain helpless and may not be in a state of mind to recognize chance opportunities. In a state of helplessness, individuals may ultimately lack the ability to exhibit proactive behaviour and responsibility for their career development. Alternatively, those who believe they have control over their future and actions will be more likely to identify chance circumstances and individuals, knowing that these factors have the potential to play a positive role in their Canadian career development. Fundamentally, these like-minded individuals will act in such a manner to attain their desired outcomes. Therefore, it is recommended that individuals learn to identify and recognize these chance opportunities, factors, and individuals (Chen, 2005). This active and positive state of mind will ultimately exhibit control over new and professional immigrants' career development experience in Canada.

Influence of Self-Efficacy among Immigrant Transition and Retraining Experience

Interestingly, the current study's findings did not illustrate self-efficacy as having as prominent of a role as optimism within immigrants' career development experience in Canada. Self-efficacy has been a primary factor within much of the career development literature and theories (SCCT) for many years. Therefore, the present researchers formulated appropriate questions that were meant to have participants reflect on their efficacy beliefs at various times throughout their transition and retraining experience. While self-efficacy undoubtedly played a role within one's Canadian career development experience, this finding was not as marked as was expected by the present researchers.

Self-Efficacy on Career Development Experience

While one's efficacy beliefs did not play as prominent of a role within immigrants' career development experience, findings nonetheless suggest the importance of one's efficacy beliefs within this domain. The majority of studies within the career development literature have focused on efficacy beliefs among ethnic and diverse populations, while only a few studies (Jerusalem & Mittag, 1995; Klassen, 2004) have focused on immigrant self-efficacy. Therefore, the present study is the first known study to qualitatively explore professional immigrants' levels of self-efficacy within a retraining program.

The present study found that the vast majority of the participants had high self-efficacy in terms of their ability to perform well within the retraining program. This is likely due to the fact that the participants in the present study were professional immigrants, and had thus already undergone formal education and training. Furthermore, the present study's findings suggest that the more efficacy an individual had, the more pleasurable they found the retraining program. High levels of self-efficacy were also found to be related with increased perception in the likelihood of attaining a job within one's area of interest (Lent, Brown, & Larkin, 1987). This was characterized by participants' expression of their confidence after the retraining program. More particularly, they felt that the retraining program provided them with relevant and valuable information, tools, and Canadian experience that were necessary to succeed in their Canadian career life. These findings are consistent with existing research on individual self-efficacy beliefs where high levels of self-efficacy have been related with increased academic and career motivation (Day & Allen, 2002; Schunk, 1991), skill development (Lent, 2005), academic performance, persistence outcomes (Lent et al., 1987; Multon, Brown, & Lent, 1991), and perceived career options (Lent et al., 1987). These are important findings for vocational and career psychology, as they provide focus on the professional immigrant population and the importance that efficacy beliefs hold in their Canadian career development.

IMPLICATIONS FOR PRACTICE

The previous discussion section revealed experiences which were representative of the professional immigrant retraining and career development experience. Factors which influenced the retraining program and overall career development experience were identified and the influence of optimism and self-efficacy within this experience were demonstrated. The findings identified primary factors within the narratives, perspectives, and behaviours of new and professional immigrants, which contribute to their current professional and personal circumstances. In addition to providing empirical support for various vocational and career psychology literature, the findings of the study have several implications for practical and theoretical directions. To allow for ease within the discussion for implications, the terms immigrants and clients are used interchangeably.

Implications for Professional Helping

This study has implications for practice in the fields of vocational psychology, counselling, career guidance and counselling, industrial and organizational psychology, and employee assistance programs. First, new and professional immigrants would benefit significantly from seeking counselling (Ishiyama & Westwood, 1992), particularly given their arduous transition process. A strong therapeutic alliance and culturally sensitive care are two primary components that should be considered the foundation for the therapeutic process (Arthur & Merali, 2005). Arthur and Merali (2005) echo the importance that the counsellor become informed and deepen his/her understanding of different multicultural groups, religions, and practices. Additionally, it is integral that the counsellor familiarize him/herself with differences in political, economical, and social practices, and how these practices may influence the immigrant's Canadian transition and overall retraining process. The nature of retraining programs differ from immigrants' general transition process, and are ultimately expected to invoke different perspectives, attitudes, feelings, and experiences. This study is one of the few studies that provides this candid insight into new and professional immigrants' retraining programs.

Important components of the therapeutic process include an awareness and understanding of the unique circumstances of each immigrant. As is evident in the present study, immigrants each experience their own complexities, stressors, and have different cognitive styles for processing such stressors and challenges. Therefore, some immigrants may feel inhibited when faced with unemployment, whereas others may perceive this as an opportunity for positive development where they engage in a retraining program. Because the present study found that many individuals were optimistic about the new Canadian experience, it is important that the counsellor does not assume that the transition process is only experienced as negative and stressful. Having this awareness, understanding, and open-minded perspective will be extremely important for counsellors dealing with new and professional immigrants.

Career Optimism and Self-Efficacy 87

Because of the uniqueness of each immigrant's experience, it is vital that each immigrant have the opportunity to tell their unique narrative within the therapeutic process. Cochran's (1997) narrative approach to career counselling has particular applicability with the present population. Within this approach, the immigrant has the ability to engage in storytelling. This provides immigrants with the opportunity to relay their past and present career development, which will aid in understanding and formulating his/her future career development (Cochran, 1997). Because the client will be discussing his/her story, the counsellor is able to gather information on what has been meaningful to the client within their career development (Sharf, 2010). There are particular techniques within this approach that can aid the client in telling their story, such as success experiences, lifelines, and life chapters. These techniques provide a particular set of tasks for the client, which can enable an open, safe, and positive environment (Cochran, 1997).

Immigrants in the present study coped with and handled their stressors and hardships in unique ways. While the present study did not emphasize coping strategies, some of the participants emphasized the importance of peer support through their transition. Additionally, the majority of the study's participants had a positive experience within their retraining program, which provided many participants with the opportunity for positive growth. Therefore, the retraining environment appears to positively influence many new and professional immigrants.

The focus on immigrants' retraining programs within the present study was emphasized due to the popularity of engaging in retraining programs (Statistics Canada, 2003). Retraining and educational programs are ideal means in helping new immigrants decipher their career development path. The vast majority of clients within the present study stated that the retraining programs increased their self-efficacy and overall confidence in their skills and abilities. Therefore, retraining programs are not only seen as a proactive means of coping with stressors such as under/unemployment, but also provide new immigrants with more confidence in themselves and their ability to secure a job.

Implications for Self-Helping

As is present in any type of change, the individual must consciously recognize his/her power and control within their current set of circumstances to allow for the desired change. Even with the help of a professional, the individual's decision to make appropriate changes (either internal or external) is the primary component in creating positive transformation. It is recognized that professional help is very limited within Canadian society, particularly for the immigrant population, as new immigrants are sometimes not aware of such services, or are not able to afford psychological or professional help. Therefore, it is integral that implications for self-help are made accessible to new and professional immigrants in Canadian society, and are thus important to discuss.

The present study's findings illustrate that the vast majority of individual work to engage in coping strategies or the decision to adopt a different attitude was self-motivated, without assistance from professionals. Many of the participants within the present study did state that the support from their family was incremental throughout their experience in Canada, on both a personal and professional level. Furthermore, most of the participants reported that their peers within the retraining program provided them with an invaluable amount of support and strength, which was significantly engendered from the ability to relate to immigrant counterparts. This importance of peer support has been present across various psychological research areas, with particular regard to the immigrant population (Foa, 1998; Heal & Jacobs, 2005; Kobayashi, 2006), as stories of familiarity in experience and struggles provide immigrants with civilization and cognizance. By socializing and relating with peers, immigrants may be better able to implement particular coping strategies, may hear of additional help or resources, and may ultimately be able to re-shape their perspectives on their current career-life circumstances.

Additional importance for immigrants includes their ability to exhibit control over their cognitive style, which is suggested by the present study to play a significant role in their perception of career-related control, ability to cope with hardships, career motivation, self-efficacy, performance, and happiness, in addition to various other positive outcomes. In learning to strengthen their cognitive style (i.e., optimism) through practice and helpful exercises, their chance in developing learned optimism will increase (Seligman, 1991).

LIMITATIONS OF THE STUDY

In considering the implications of the study for practice and policy, it is important to recognize the present study's limitations. The generalizability of the study's findings may be limited by a number of weaknesses, the most significant being that the present study's participants were primarily made up of males. In particular, the present study included 10 participants, with 7 of them being male, and only 3 of them female. One may expect differences among individual levels of optimism and self-efficacy, and their influence on one's career-life experience in Canada. It may be therefore argued that the findings are only reflective of cognitive style, perspectives, beliefs, and actions of males. Thus, it cannot be assumed that most new and professional immigrants share the same characteristics and experiences that were present within the participants of this study. Therefore, future research is advised to consider including an equal number of male and female participants, which will allow for further generalizability. In addition, the present study did not include particular questions on individual levels of optimism, yet judged individual cognitive style and optimism levels on existing definitions and characteristics (Seligman, 1991). It can therefore be argued that the present study did not use a measurable means in defining one's cognitive style, regardless of the fact that importance of optimism and attitude were spontaneously brought into conversation by the majority of the participants.

SUGGESTIONS FOR FUTURE RESEARCH

The study of professional immigrant retraining and career development is still in its infancy. The paucity of research on the characteristics, influence of optimism and self-efficacy, and individual beliefs leave significant room for future researchers. There is an abundance of opportunities for researchers to focus on a wide range of variables within this area. It is the hope of this researcher that the present research will lay the groundwork for future studies exploring new and professional immigrants' retraining experiences in Canada, with a particular focus on the influence of optimism and self-efficacy.

Because this is a preliminary study, it would be beneficial to conduct similar in-depth research among professional immigrants as a means of determining consistency. In particular, it is important that researchers demonstrate consistency for the presence of optimism and self-efficacy as influencing cognitive styles on successful retraining and career development experiences. An interesting finding of the present study was optimists' perceived control over their personal and professional lives, in contrast with pessimists' greater attribution on the importance of chance within their experiences. Future research should consider exploring these relationships on a more in-depth level. In particular, this exploration would benefit from both quantitative and qualitative methodologies. A combination of objective and subjective methodologies may be able to provide a more transparent link between optimists and control for career development, and pessimists' locus of control within their career development. Such information would provide both career and positive psychology research with an abundance of information and implications for practice, theory, and research.

Career counselling research could additionally benefit from the exploration of coping strategies, with a particular focus on self-talk. Some of the present study's participants revealed that they effectively coped with various barriers and hardships, yet did not provide an in-depth perspective into such coping strategies. Because the study was particularly interested in optimists' experience in overcoming hardships, it is presumed that practical coping mechanisms were used, in addition to self-talk, or cognitive reframing. In exploring new immigrants' coping strategies, research would be able to provide newcomers with additional techniques and strategies that will alleviate distress and ease their overall transition and hardships experienced in Canada.

CONCLUSION

The previous section included directions for future research, given the present study's findings and their associated implications. Immigrants who participated in the present study undoubtedly experienced barriers and hardships within their transition to Canada and their Canadian retraining experience. However, the present study sought to uncover how immigrants' optimism and self-efficacy influence their ability to cope with these hardships, their transition process, and retraining program. Overall, the process of immigration and the retraining experience for professional immigrants was a positive one. Through the use of in-depth interviews, the present study found that optimism positively influenced individuals' retraining experiences, as well as their fulfillment and satisfaction within their personal and professional lives. Additionally, optimists were better able to cope with unforeseen stressors and challenges, wherein they exhibited characteristics of resiliency. Lastly, optimists also perceived having more choice and control over their career-life experiences in Canada. Alternatively, immigrants who were identified as pessimists experienced a more negative retraining experience, struggled significantly when they were faced with challenges, and believed they had little or no control in regards to their career-life experiences and their future career development. The present study also found that retraining programs positively impacted immigrants' self-efficacy and overall confidence in their abilities and skills in Canada. Furthermore, immigrants who had high levels of self-efficacy had a more pleasant retraining experience, and had an increased belief in their ability to attain a job within their area of expertise. To conclude, the present study serves as a preliminary step towards the importance and focus on growth, positive development, and optimism among the new and professional immigrant population. Ultimately, this study hopes to serve as a proactive step that will engender a healthier frame of mind and an overall positive career-life experience for new and professional immigrants in Canada.

REFERENCES

Adachi, T. (2001). Career development by university students: Social cognitive career theory. *Japanese Journal of Educational Psychology, 49* (4), 326-336.

Ali, S. R., & Saunders, J. L. (2006). College expectations of rural Appalachian youth: An exploration of social cognitive career theory factors. *The Career Development Quarterly, 55*(1), 38-51.

Amundson, N. E., Borgen, W. A., & Reuter, J. (2004). Using portfolios to enhance career resilience. *Journal of Employment Counseling, 41*(2), 50-59.

Arthur, N., & Merali, N. (2005). *Counselling immigrants and refugees.* In N. Arthur & S. Collins (Eds.). Culture-infused counselling: Celebrating the Canadian mosaic, 337-360.

Bandura, A. (2001). Social cognitive theory: An agentic perspective. *Annual review of psychology, 52*(1), 1-26.

Bauder, H. (2003). 'Brain Abuse' or the devaluation of immigrant labour in Canada. *Antipode,* 35 (4), 700-717.

Beltrame, J. (2012). Canadian labour market weakest in non-slump periods in decades, CIBC says. Retrieved February 11, 2012, from http://www.canadianbusiness.com/article/67528-canadian-labour-market-weakest-in-non-slump-periods-in-decades-cibc-says.

Berry, J. W. (2001). A Psychology of Immigration. *Journal of Social Issues, 57*(3), 615-631.

Betz, N. E. (2000). Self-efficacy as a basis for career assessment. *Journal of Career Assessment, 8*(8), 205-222.

Betz, N. E., & Hackett, G. (1981). The relationship of career-related self-efficacy expectations to perceived career options in college women and men. *Journal of Counseling Psychology, 28*(5), 399-410.

Beynon, J., Ilieva, R., & Dichupa, M. (2004). Re-credentialling experiences of immigrant teachers: negotiating institutional structures, professional identities and pedagogy. *Teachers and Teaching, 10*(4), 429-444.

Blumer, H. (1931). Science without concepts. *American Journal of Sociology, 36*(4), 515-533.

Brouwer, A. (1999). *Immigrants need not apply* (pp. 1-18). Ottawa: Caledon Institute of Social Policy.

Bryant, A. (2002). Re-grounding grounded theory. *Journal of Information Technology Theory and Application, 4*(1), 25-42.

Camarota, S. A., & Jensenius, K. (2009). Trends in Immigrant and Native Employment. *Centre for Immigration Studies*, 1-21.

Canada Immigration Lawyers. (2011). *CanadaVisa.Com*. Retrieved August 11, 2011, from http://www.canadavisa.com/proving-english-language-ability-ielts.html.

Canada Updates. (2009). *Canada Updates*. Retrieved June 27, 2011, from http://www.canada.updates.com.

Canadian Labour and Business Centre. (2003). Labour Market Integration: Issues and Challenges for New Immigrants. Retrieved August 6, 2008, from http://www.clbc.ca/files/Reports/HB_section_c.pdf.

Chang, A. (2006). Ethnic identity and social cognitive determinants of Korean American career choices in the science and non-science domains. *Dissertation Abstracts International Section A: Humanities and Social Sciences, 67*(3-A), 835.

Charlotte-Mecklenburg Workforce Development Board, & Morris, C. (2002). *Cultural and Language Barriers in the Workplace*. Charlotte-Mecklenburg Workforce Development Board.

References

Charmaz, K. (2006). *Constructing grounded theory: a practical guide through qualitative analysis.* Thousand Oaks, CA: Sage Publications, *9*(1), 125-129.

Charmaz, K., & Mitchell, R. G. (1996). The myth of silent authorship: Self, substance, and style in ethnographic writing. *Symbolic Interaction, 19*(4), 285-302.

Chen, C. P. (2004). Positive compromise: A new perspective for career psychology. *Australian Journal of Career Development, 13*(2), 17-28.

Chen, C. P. (2005). Understanding career chance. *International Journal for Educational and Vocational Guidance, 5*(3), 251-270.

Chen, C. P. (2006). *Career endeavour: Pursuing a cross-cultural life transition.* Ashgate Publishing, Ltd.

Chen, C. P. (2008). Career guidance with immigrants. In *International handbook of career guidance* (pp. 419-442). Springer Netherlands.

Chen, C. P., & Lee, W. (2011). *Ethnicity and careers of Chinese-Canadian young adults.* New York: Nova Science Publishers.

Citizenship and Immigration Canada (CIC), 2007. Skilled workers and professionals. *CIC.* Retrieved January 11, 2012, from http://www.cic.gc.ca/english/immigrate/skilled/index.asp.

Citizenship and Immigration Canada. (2009). Canada Facts and Figures. *CIC.* Immigrant Overview: Permanent and Temporary Residents. Retrieved on January 6, 2011, from http://www.cic.gc.ca/english/pdf/research-stats/facts2009.pdf.

Clarke, A. E. (2003). Situational analyses: Grounded theory mapping after the postmodern turn. *Symbolic interaction, 26*(4), 553-576.

Clement, R., Noels, K. A., & Deneault, B. (2001). Interethnic contact, identity, and psychological adjustment: The mediating and moderating roles of communication. *Journal of Social Issues, 57*(3), 559-577.

Cochran, L. (1990). *The sense of vocation: A study of career and life development.* SUNY Press.

Cochran, L. (1997). *Career counseling: A narrative approach.* Sage.

Cohen-Goldner, S., & Eckstein Z. (2008). Labor Mobility of Immigrants: Training, Experience, Language, and Opportunities. *International Economic Review, 449*(3), 837-872.

Corbin, J., & Strauss, A. (1990). Grounded Theory Research: Procedures, Canons, and Evaluative Criteria. *Zeitschridt fur Soziologie, 19*(6), 418-427.

Creed, P., Patton, W., & Bartrum, D. (2002). Multidimensional Properties of the Lot-R: Effects of Optimism and Pessimism on Career and Well-Being Related Variables in Adolescents. *Journal of Career Assessment, 10*(1), 42-61.

Day, R. & Allen, T. D. (2002). The relationship between career motivation and self-efficacy with protégé career success. *Journal of Vocational Behavior, 64*(1), 72-91.

De Vita, G. (2001). Learning Styles, Culture and Inclusive Instruction in the Multicultural Classroom: A Business and Management Perspective. *Innovations in Education and Teaching International, 38*(2), 165 -174.

Dean, J. A., & Wilson, K. (2009). 'Education? It is irrelevant to my job now. It makes me very depressed...': Exploring the health impacts of under/unemployment among highly skilled recent immigrants in Canada. *Ethnicity & Health, 14*(2), 185-204.

Dewey, J. (1925). *Experience and Nature.* Chicago: Open Court.

Foa, E. B., & Rothbaum, B. O. (2001). *Treating the trauma of rape: Cognitive-behavioral therapy for PTSD.* Guilford Press.

Fontaine, K. R., Manstead, A. S. R., & Wagner, H. (2006). Optimism, perceived control over stress, and coping. *European Journal of Personality, 7*(4), 267-281.

Glaser, B. G. (1999). The Future of Grounded Theory. *Qualitative Health Research, 9*(6), 836-845.

Globe and Mail. (1996a). Skilled immigrants meet job barriers: more trained people than ever are coming in but bureaucrats are not ready to handle them. *Globe and Mail.* November 19, p.A1, A6.

Globe and Mail. (1996b). Dentists alarmed by paradental surge: foreign trained professionals unable to get licenses in Ontario launch own practices. *Globe and Mail.* November 19, p.A6.

Globe and Mail. (1996c). Screening of foreign doctors criticized. *Globe and Mail.* December 16, p.A8.

References

Gorbatova, R., & Eaglstein, A. S. (1998). Professional retraining of highly educated immigrant professionals. *International Social Work, 41*(4), 239-253.

Gudykunst, W. B., & Hammer, M. R. (1988). Strangers and hosts: An uncertainty reduction based theory of intercultural adaptation. *Cross-cultural adaptation: Current approaches, 11*, 106-139.

Gushue, G. V. (2006). The relationship of ethnic identity, career decision-making self-efficacy and outcome expectations among Latino/a high school students. *Journal of Vocational Behavior, 68*(1) 85-95.

Gushue, G. V., & Whitson, M. L. (2006). The relationship among support, ethnic identity, career decision self-efficacy, and outcome expectations in African American high school students: Applying social cognitive career theory. *Journal of Career Development, 33*(2), 112-124.

Hackett, G., & Betz, N. (1981). A self-efficacy approach to the career development of women. *Journal of Vocational Behavior, 18*, 326-339.

Hackett, G., & Lent, R. W. (1992). Theoretical advances and current inquiry in career psychology. *Handbook of counseling psychology, 2*, 419-452.

Hagevik, S. (1998). Resilience required. *Journal of Environmental Health, 60*(10), 37(32)-39.

Hartung, P. J., Vandiver, B. J., Leong, F. T. L., Pope, M., Niles, S. G., & Farrow, B. (1998). Appraising cultural identity in career-development assessment and counseling. *The Career Development Quartlerly, 46*(3), 276-293.

Heal, C. & Jacobs, H. (2005). A peer support program for international medical graduates. *Australian Family Physician, 34*(4), 276-278.

Herr, E. L., & Cramer, S. H. (1988). *Career guidance and counseling through the life span: Systematic approaches.* Scott, Foresman & Co.

Hofstede, G. (1984). The Cultural Relativity of the Quality of Life Concept. *The Academy of Management Review, 9*(3), 389-398.

Hongxia, S. (2009). Shaping the Re-Training and Re-Education Experiences of Immigrant Women: The Credential and Certificate Regime in Canada. *International Journal of Lifelong Education, 28*(3), 353-369.

Hughes, E. C. (1971). *The sociological eye: Selected papers.* Transaction publishers.

Ishiyama, F. I., & Westwood, M. J. (1992). Enhancing client-validating communication: helping discouraged clients in cross-cultural adjustment. *Journal of Multicultural Counseling and Development, 20*, 50-63.

Jafari, S., Baharlou, S., & Mathias, R. (2010). Knowledge of Determinants of Mental Health among Iranian Immigrants of BC, Canada: "A Qualitative Study." *Immigrant Minority Health, 12*, 100-106.

Jerusalem, M., & Mittag, W. (1995). Self-efficacy in stressful life transitions. *Self-efficacy in changing societies*, 177-201.

Kaniel, R., Massey, C., & Robinson, D. T. (2010). *The importance of being an optimist: Evidence from labor markets* (No. w16328). National Bureau of Economic Research.

Karademas, E. (2006). Self-efficacy, social support, and well-being: The mediating role of optimism. *Personality and Individual Differences, 40*(6), 1281-1290.

King, A. Y., & Bond, M. H. (1985). The Confucian paradigm of man: A sociological view. In *Chinese culture and mental health* (pp. 29-45).

Kirkbride, P. S., Tang, S. F., Y., & Ko, G. (1989). *Emigration from Hong Kong: Evidence from organisations.* Hong Kong Institute of Personnel Management, City Polytechnic of Hong Kong.

Klassen, R. M. (2004). Optimism and realism: A review of self-efficacy from a cross-cultural perspective. *International Journal of Psychology, 39*(3), 205-230.

Kobayashi, M. (2006). The role of peer support in ESL students' accomplishment of oral academic tasks. *Canadian modern language review, 10*, 337-369.

Lamb, M. (2009). Half empty? Half full? *Redbook, 212*(4), 158.

Lau, V. P., & Shaffer, M. A. (1999). Career success: the effects of personality. *Career Development International, 4*(4), 225 - 231.

Lazarus, R. S. (1991). *Emotion and adaptation.* Oxford University Press on Demand.

Lee, B. K., Fong, M., & Solowoniuk, J. (2007). Transplanted Lives: Immigration Challenges and Pathological Gambling Among Four Canadian Chinese Immigrants. *Immigrant Stress, 1*-19.

References

Lee, H. S., Brown, S., Mitchell, M., & Shiraldi, G. (2008). Correlates of Resilience in the Face of Adversity for Korean Women Immigrating to the US. *Immigrant Minority Health, 10*, 415-422.

Lent, R. W. (2005). *A Social Cognitive View of Career Development and Counseling.*

Lent, R. W., Brown, S. D., & Hackett, G. (1993). Toward a unified social cognitive theory of career and academic interest, choice, and performance. *Journal of Vocational Behavior*, 45, 79-122.

Lent, R. W., Brown, S. D., & Larkin, K. C. (1987). Comparison of three theoretically derived variables in predicting career and academic behavior: Self-efficacy, interest congruence, and consequence thinking. *Journal of Counseling Psychology, 34*(3), 292-298.

Lent, R. W., Brown, S. D., Nota, L., & Soresi, S. (2003). Testing social cognitive interest and choice hypotheses across Holland types in Italian high school students. *Journal of Vocational Behavior, 62*, 101-118.

Lochhead, C. (2003). *The transition penalty: Unemployment among recent immigrants to Canada: CLBC commentary.* Canadian Labour and Business Centre.

Lounsbury, J. W., Park, S. H., Sundstrom, E., Williamson, J. M., & Pemberton, A. E. (2004). Personality, Career Satisfaction, and Life Satisfaction: Test of a Directional Model. *Journal of Career Assessment, 12*(4), 395-406.

Lum, L. (2009). *Accommodating Learning Styles in Bridging Education Programs for Internationally Educated Professionals.* Canadian Council on Learning, 1-35. Retrieved February 1, 2012, from http://www.ccl-cca.ca/pdfs/fundedresearch/Lum-FinalReport.pdf.

Luzzo, D. A., & McWhirter, E. H. (2001). Sex and ethnic differences in the perception of educational and career-related barriers and levels of coping efficacy. *Journal of Counseling & Development, 79*, 61-67.

Lyubomirsky, S. (2001). Why are some people happier than others? The role of cognitive and motivational processes in well-being. *American Psychologist, 56*(3), 239-249.

Mak, A. S., Westwood, M. J., & Ishiyama, I. F. (1994). Developing role-based social competencies for career search and development in Hong Kong immigrants. *Journal of Career Development, 20*(3), 171-183.

Mak, A., Westwood, M., & Ishiyama, I. (1994). Developing Role-Based Social Competencies for Career Search and Development in Hong Kong immigrants. *Journal of Career Development, 20*(3), 171-183.

Maxwell, J. A. (2012). *Qualitative research design: An interactive approach* (Vol. 41). Sage publications.

Mead, G. H. (1934). *Mind, Self, and Society.* Chicago: University of Chicago.

Mishel, M. H., Hostetter, T., King, B., & Graham, V. (1984). Predictors of psychosocial adjustment in patients newly diagnosed with gynecological cancer. *Cancer Nursing, 7*(4), 281-348.

Mitchell, L., Levin, A., & Krumboltz, J. (1999). Planned happenstance: Constructing unexpected career opportunities. *Journal of Counseling and Development, 77*, 115-124.

Multon, K. D., Brown, S. D., & Lent, R. (1991). Relation of self-efficacy beliefs to academic outcomes: A meta-analytic investigation. *Journal of Counseling Psychology, 38*(1), 30-38.

Neimark, J. (1987). *The Power of Positive Thinkers.* Retrieved on March 10, 2012, from http://3000thoughts.com/wp-content/uploads/2011/10/The-Power-of-Positive-Thinkers.pdf.

Neto, F. (1995). Predictors of satisfaction with life among 2nd-generation migrants. *Social Indicators Research, 35*(1), 93-116.

Nidoo, J. C. (1992). The mental health of visible ethnic minorities in Canada. *Psychology and Developing Societies, 4*(2), 87-165.

O'Campo, P., Eaton, W., & Muntaner, C. (2004). Labour market experience, work organization, gender inequalities and health status: results form a prospective analysis of US employed women. *Social Science & Medicine, 58*, 585-594.

Park, R., & Burgess, E. (1921). *An Introduction to the Science of Sociology,* Chicago: The University of Chicago Press.

References

Patton, W., Bartrum, D., & Creed, P. A. (2002). The role of optimism and career locus of control in predicting career related behaviours. *The Career Development Quarterly, 49*, 336-351.

Peterson, C. (2000). The future of optimism. *American psychologist, 55*(1), 44.

Pew Research Centre (1999). *Optimism Reigns, Technology Plays Key Role.* Retrieved January 27, 2012, from http://www.people-press.org/1999/10/24/optimism-reigns-technology-plays-key-role/.

Pew Research Centre. (2006). *Once Again, the Future Ain't What It Used To Be.* Retrieved September 17, 2011, from http://pewresearch.org/assets/social/pdf/BetterOff.pdf.

Pottie, K. (2007). Misinterpretation. Language proficiency, recent immigrants, and global health disparities. *Canadian Family Physician, 53*, 1899-1901.

Rasmussen, H., Wrosch, C., Scheier, M., & Carver, C. (2006). Self-regulation processes and health: The importance of optimism and goal adjustment. *Journal of Personality, 74*, 1721-1747.

Rastogi, M. (2007). Coping with Transitions in Asian Indian Families: Systemic Clinical Interventions with Immigrants. *Journal of Systemic Therapies, 26*(2), 55-67.

Reitz, J. (2001). Immigrant Skill Utilization in the Canadian Labour Market: Implications of Human Capital Research. *Journal of International Migration and Integration, 2*(3), 347-378.

Riolli, L., Savicki, V., & Cepani, A. (2002). Resilience in the face of catastrophe: Optimism, personality and coping in the Kosovo crisis. *Journal of Applied Social Psychology, 32*(8), 1604-1627.

Rottinghaus, P. J., Day, S. X., & Borgen, F. H. (2005). The Career Futures Inventory: A Measure of Career-Related Adaptability and Optimism. *Journal of Career Assessment, 13*(1), 3-24.

Ruiz, R. (2010). Undocumented immigrants offer U.S. a shot of optimism. *CNN.* Retrieved August 1, 2011, from http://articles.cnn.com/2010-03-09/opinion/ruiz.immigration.optimism_1_immigrants-national-poverty-rate-living?_s=PM:OPINION.

Schunk, D. H. (1991). Self-efficacy and academic motivation. *Educational Psychologist, 26*, 207-231.

Schwarzer, R., & Luszczynska, A. (2007). *Self-efficacy*. In M. Gerrard & K.D. McCaul (Eds.) Health Behavior Constructs: Theory, Measurement, and Research. National Cancer Institute. Retrieved from http://cancercontrol.cancer.gov/constructs.

Schyns, B. (2001). The Relationship between employees' self-monitoring and occupational self-efficacy and transformational leadership. *Current Research in Social Psychology, 7*, 30-42.

Schyns, B. (2004). The Influence of Occupational Self-Efficacy on the Relationship of Leadership Behavior and Preparedness for Occupational Change. *Journal of Career Development, 30*(4), 247-261.

Scott, E. (2011). *The benefits of optimism*. Staying positive can improve stress management, productivity, and your health. Retrieved June 14, 2011, from http://stress.about.comod/optimismspirituality/a/optimism benefit.htm.

Seale, C. (1999). *The quality of qualitative research*. London: Sage Publications.

Seligman, M. E. P. (1972). Learned helplessness. *Annual Review of Medicine, 23*, 407-412.

Seligman, M. E. P. (1991*). Learned Optimism: How to Change Your Mind and Your Life*. New York. ISBN 0-671-01911-2.

Seligman, M. E. P. (1995). *What you can change and what you can't: The complete guide to successful self-improvement*. New York: Ballantine Books.

Seligman, M., & Lee, Y. T. (1997). Are Americans More Optimistic Than the Chinese? *The Society for Personality and Social Psychology, 23*(1), 32-40.

Sharf, R. S. (2016). *Applying career development theory to counseling*. Nelson Education.

Shea, C. M., & Howell, J. M. (1999). Charismatic leadership and task feedback: A laboratory study of their effects on self-efficacy and task performance. *Leadership Quarterly, 10*, 375-396.

References 103

Shein, J. L., & Chen, C. P. (2011). *Work-Family enrichment: A research of positive transfer*. Rotterdam, The Netherlands: Sense Publishers.

Statistics Canada (2003). Longitudinal Survey of Immigrants to Canada. *Statistics Canada*. Retrieved September 15, 2010, from http://www.statcan.gc.ca/daily-quotidien/030904/dq030904a-eng.htm.

Statistics Canada (2005). Earnings and Incomes of Canadians Over the Past Quarter Century, 2006 Census: Earnings. Gap in earnings widens between recent immigrants and Canadian-born workers. *Statistics Canada*. Retrieved January 3, 2012, from http://www12.statcan.ca/census-recensement/2006/as-sa/97-563/p13-eng.cfm.

Statistics Canada (2007a). Study: Canada's immigrant labour market. *Statistics Canada*. Retrieved July 24, 2011, from http://www.statcan.gc.ca/daily-quotidien/ 070910/dq070910a-eng.htm.

Statistics Canada (2007b). Chronic Low Income and Low-Income Dynamics among Recent immigrants. *Statistics Canada*. Retrieved on July 24, 2011, from http://www.statcan.gc.ca/pub/11f0019m/11f0019m2007294-eng.htm.

Statistics Canada (2008). Literacy skills among Canada's immigrant population. *Statistics Canada*. Retrieved September 10, 2010, from http://www.statcan.gc.ca/pub/81-004-x/2005005/9112-eng.htm.

Statistics Canada (2010). http://www.statcan.gc.ca/pub/91-002-x/2010003/aftertoc-aprestdm1-eng.htm Retrieved on February 24, 2011.

Strauss, A. & Corbin, J. (1990). *Basics of qualitative research: Grounded theory procedures and techniques*. Newbury Park, CA: Sage Publications.

Super, D. E. (1990). *A life-span, life-space approach to career development*. In D. Brown & L. Brooks (Eds.), Career choice and development: Applying contemporary theories to practice (2nd ed., pp. 197-261). San Francisco: Jossey-Bass.

Thompson, J. B. (1981). *Critical hermeneutics. Cambridge: Cambridge University Press*. Toronto Star (1995). Degrees don't mean jobs for Third World professionals. June 17, p.A2.

Waller, B. (2006). Math interest and choice intentions of non-traditional African American college students. *Journal of Vocational Behavior, 68*(3), 538-547.

Ward, C., Bochner, S., & Furnham, A. (2001). *The psychology of culture shock (2nd ed.)*. New York, NY: Routledge.

Weiss, K. I. (2001). The social cognitive model of career choice: A cross-cultural analysis (Doctoral dissertation, State University of New York at Buffalo, 2001). *Dissertation Abstracts International: Section B, 61*(9-B), 6502.

Wilkins, R., Berthelot, J. M. & Ng, E. (2002). Trends in mortality by neighbourhood income in urban Canada from 1971 to 1986. *Health Reports, 13*, 45-71.

Zaharna, R. S. (1989). Self-shock: The double-binding challenge of identity. *International Journal of Intercultural Relations, 13*, 501-525.

APPENDIX: INTERVIEW QUESTIONS

RE: How retraining affects re-entry: Immigrants' vocational well-being

Demographic Information

1. Gender:

2. Age (in years)

3. Month and Year arriving in Canada:
   From – home country _____
   Immigrated with: Spouse ___ Family ___
   Close contact in Canada prior to immigrating? (state relationship:
   e.g., friend, cousin, etc.) _____

4. Level of Education obtained before coming to Canada
   (e.g., college education, bachelor's degree, professional certificate,
   etc.): _____

5. Please specify the Major/Discipline of your education from your
   home country (i.e., arts, science, engineering, commerce, etc.):
   _____

Degree or type of retraining completed after coming to Canada:
-Institution _____
-Program length _____
-Type of qualification/credential _____
-Type of document (Diploma/certificate/degree) _____

6. Please indicate your professional and/or vocational title before coming to Canada (e.g., teacher, nurse, engineer, accountant, etc.):

_____

7. Please indicate your **industry:** _____
Please specify your workplace **setting** in your home country (i.e., school, hospital, factory, accounting firm, etc.):

_____

8. Please indicate the job title and/or the employment you are currently holding in Canada:

_____

Please specify how long you have been working in this employment:

_____

Date of interview: _____

Questions:

I. Before Coming to Canada

(1) I'd like to ask you about your education experience.
 a) What was the name of your degree?
 b) How many years was your degree?
 c) Was there a practical component to your degree?
 d) Was there a registration component to your profession?

Appendix: Interview Questions 107

(2) I'm going to ask you some questions about your life and work experiences before coming to Canada.

a) What was your job like before you came to Canada?
b) How satisfied were you with your career prior to coming to Canada?
c) Things you liked and didn't like?
d) How central was your career to your sense of self?

(3) Why did you want to come to Canada, and how did you make this decision to come?
--Reason(s), and main purpose.
--Events and experiences and information that triggered your decision

(4) (If not answered already) Was employment and worklife involved in your decision of immigration? (and how) What were your expectations for employment in Canada? (if not already answered) How confident did you feel about finding work in your profession?

Did you do any preparation for your qualifications to be transferable to Canada before coming to Canada?--(If not already answered) Can you tell me about your preparation and planning for employment in Canada?

(5) How much control did you feel you would have in Canada over employment decisions?

(6) Did you anticipate or plan on having to do retraining once you arrived in Canada?

(7) If yes, did you do any planning for your retraining prior to coming to Canada? What planning did you do?

(8) What were your expectations of the retraining process? What did you think the experience would be like?

II. After Coming to Canada: Initial General Experience

(1) How did you feel when you initially came to Canada? (Were things different than your expectations/what you expected?)

(2) What were the most significant changes and difficulties you experienced when you first came to Canada?

> a) How did you cope with the changes and difficulties in life?
> b) What was most helpful, least helpful for coping with these changes?
> c) How did these experiences impact your well-being? (mental and physical health), and the well-being of your family?

(3) How did your ability to cope with these changes impact your self-esteem and confidence levels?

(4) Did you search for help or resources? If so, what were they?

(5) Having faced these difficulties/changes, did you develop a plan of action for your career development? Did that include plans for retraining?

III. Ongoing Vocational Adjustment and Transition in Canada

(1) How important was it for you to find a job when you first came to Canada? Which kind of jobs did you intend to find to get your worklife restarted in Canada?

(2) (If not already answered, Cover all of these points) What were the major factors you had to consider when you were trying to find employment in Canada?
> -- Concerns for financial survival.
> -- Gain Canadian experience.
> -- Some relevancy to previous educational and professional background experience.

Appendix: Interview Questions 109

(3) What did you do to try to get a job that is related to your previous vocational and/or professional background experience from your home country? (Use discretion). -if applicable.

(4) Could you tell me briefly in sequential order the main jobs you have held since coming to this country, and your experiences with these jobs?

(5) Was there a period of time during which you were unemployed after coming to Canada? For how long? How did this affect you?

(6) How difficult or easy was your original job search? What factors made the search easier and/or more difficult?

(7) What were some of the expected and unexpected events that influenced your job-seeking and vocational development experiences in Canada? And how did you respond to such events?
    --Opportunities/people that led you to a vocational choice
    --Anticipated or unanticipated barriers.
    a) What was most helpful, least helpful to you?

(7) What were some of the supports you found in your job search in Canada? Could you give me some specific examples?

(8) In your job-search in Canada, how useful was your work experience from your home country?

(9) Were your qualifications and training from your home country useful in getting work?

(10) How long after you came to Canada did you decide to pursue retraining/ further education? What led to that decision? What factors influenced this decision? Did anyone influence your decision?

(11) What had you hoped your retraining or education in Canada would lead to?

(12) How did you plan for your retraining? Did you encounter any barriers in this process?

(13) What actions did you take to make your retraining experience possible?
-- What resources did you seek out? Did anyone help you?

(14) (If not already answered) How did you find out about available retraining opportunities? (career centre, internet, social network, job etc. ...)

(15) What form of retraining or professional training did you do once you arrived in Canada?
-- Did you try to regain your pre-Canada professional qualification/designation?

(16) In what field was your retraining? How did you choose the program/field?
--Why did you stay in the same field? OR Why did you change fields?
-- If you changed fields, how did you come to the decision to change?

(17) How did you find this new "learning" experience in Canada? Did you have to change your "learning style"? In what ways?

(18) Could you describe your general impression and feeling about this training experience?
--Things you enjoyed the most.
--Things you enjoyed the least.

(19) How did the retraining compare to your original training back home?

(20) Did the retraining experience differ from what you expected it would be like?

(21) If different how did it affect you? How did you cope?

Appendix: Interview Questions 111

(22) (If not already touched on) Were there any unexpected or chance events that occurred prior to, during, and after your retraining?
-- Any unexpected events that occurred that led you to take the training program?
-- Any unexpected learning experiences?
-- Any unexpected benefits or costs from retraining?

(23) How much control (or lack of control) did you feel you had in terms of your retraining experience? (ref for interviewer e.g., choice of institute, choice of certificate, ability to re- accredit in your old field vs. being forced to retrain for something completely new, limitations of funding sources or finances for training, etc...).
a) What led to this feeling and what did you do in response to it?

(24) Thinking about your pre-Canada skills and abilities, how did you think you would perform in the retraining? (interviewer: thinking about self-efficacy)

(25) How did you feel about having to take this retraining? (e.g., resentment for the necessity of retraining vs. framing it as a new opportunity, positive chance for growth vs. feeling lucky that retraining was a possibility...)-interviewer give both sides of possibility.

(26) What were some sources of support for you during your retraining experience? (e.g., family, classmates, mentors, friends, etc...)

(27) What was the role of your interests or hobbies in coping with your retraining experience?
How do these activities help you cope? (e.g., losing yourself, engaging)

(28) Were you employed during your retraining experience? Which role? What was it like having to balance both? Do you feel it impacted your retraining?

IV. Results of Post-Retraining

(1) How important and useful was your Canadian retraining experience to your employment opportunities in this country?
> --Leading to employment that was similar or close to your background experience.
> --Leading to new vocational choice and opportunity.
> --Leading to no beneficial outcome for employment.

(2) What is your understanding of why it became necessary for you to pursue retraining in Canada?

(3) (For those of you who re-trained in your original career), do you agree that the retraining was necessary for you to be competent in your profession after arriving here in Canada?

(4) How did you feel about your skills and abilities after the training program? (Did you feel better or discouraged about yourself, the same?)

(5) How did the process of retraining affect (or not affect) your sense of "career identity"?
> (Sense of yourself or experience of yourself as ___profession)
> a) Did your sense of identity evolve during your retraining experience (identity at the beginning vs. middle vs. end)?
> b) What impact does this experience have on your perception of self-worthiness as a new Canadian?

(6) Has your career taken on a different role in your life as a result of your retraining experience?
> -- Has your career identity changed as a result of your retraining experience?

(7) During the retraining, what did you discover about yourself? (Prompt: Self-discovery and meaning on a personal career-related level)

Appendix: Interview Questions 113

(8) Did your retraining lead you to be more encouraged or discouraged to pursue your desired career? How come?

(9) How did the retraining program impact the factors that motivate you within your career? Did your career-related values change? (e.g., enjoyment of work and interest in professional activities vs. importance of prestige, salary, promotion) If so, how so?

(10) Is there anything else that you feel you gained or lost through retraining?

(11) What were some of the main lessons you learned from your retraining experience in Canada?

(12) Was the retraining what you expected it to be? If not, how did it differ? What issues did this raise? How did you feel about those issues? What did you do about those issues?

(13) How did any difference in expectations versus the reality of your retraining affect your sense of identity or value as a person, your confidence levels, and feelings in terms of your career?

(14) What were the major compromises you made when approaching retraining opportunities in Canada? How did you decide what to do when you had to make a compromise in your retraining? (Joint action - family, mentor, community)

(15) How did you feel when you had to make a compromise for your retraining choice?

(16) In general, how has your retraining impacted your experience as a new worker in Canada?

(17) How important were your own actions in setting up and completing your retraining?

(18) After your retraining, what did you do to build your career in Canada? (Steps toward current employment... see next section)

V. Current Employment

(1)   Could you tell me about the circumstances that led you to your present work life?
--The nature of your employment.

(2) How do you feel about your current job? Could you tell me the things you like and/or dislike about your current employment?

(3) How does the employment you hold now compare to the employment you held prior to moving to Canada?

(4) How important is your vocational life in your total new life in Canada? How does your work life affect your personal and family life here?

(5) Do you feel a sense of vocational and career identity from your current employment experience in Canada? Why or why not?

(6) Do you feel that some of your qualifications (e.g., hard and soft skills) or strengths are not being used in your work-life? For example, do you have skills that are not used in your job?
What needs to change for your skills to be better utilized? (e.g., actions you can take, actions your employer or the system can take)

(7) Overall, what factors have been the most influential in helping you to succeed in your career development within Canada? What factors have made your career life difficult?

(8) Have any factors challenged your beliefs that you could succeed in your career/work-life?

(9) How satisfied do you feel about your career/work-life experience in Canada?

Appendix: Interview Questions 115

(10) Consider your life as it has turned out until now, how much of an element of choice has there been? For example, is the job you do a chosen vocation or more or less the result of a series of chance events? Are there any aspects of your life that are the result of a considered choice?

(11) What has the role of chance been in your life and career in Canada? What did you do in response to chance events?
    a) How do you feel about the chance events in your life?

(12) What are some of your main concerns and needs about your future worklife in Canada? How do you feel about your future vocational development prospects in Canada, and why do you feel this way?

(13) Do you intend or expect to pursue any additional retraining in the future? Why or why not?
    What type?

(14) What will you intend to do to improve the quality of your work-life and to enhance your career development in Canada?

(15) Anticipate your vocational direction 5 years from now.
    a) How have your career priorities changed?

(16) What are some of the most important career-related lessons you learned and looking back, is there anything that you would have done differently?

INDEX

A

Acculturative Stress, 16
Achievement, 12, 22, 76
Anxiety/ Stress, 3, 7, 10, 12, 14, 15, 16, 21, 23, 29, 50, 61, 66, 76, 77, 78, 96, 98, 102
Appraisal Style, 20
Attribution Theory, 20

B

Bandura, 5, 24, 25, 69, 93
Betz, 24, 25, 94, 97

C

Career, i, iii, ix, 1, 3, 4, 5, 6, 7, 9, 10, 11, 12, 14, 15, 16, 18, 19, 20, 21, 23, 24, 25, 26, 27, 28, 31, 32, 33, 37, 38, 40, 41, 45, 46, 47, 56, 57, 58, 59, 60, 61, 62, 63, 64, 65, 66, 67, 68, 73, 74, 75, 76, 77, 78, 79, 80, 82, 83, 84, 85, 86, 87, 88, 89, 90, 91, 93, 94, 95, 96, 97, 98, 99, 100, 101, 102, 103, 104, 107, 108, 110, 112, 113, 114, 115
And Optimism, 101
And Pessimism, 96
Career Development, 4, 21, 60, 68, 75, 79, 84, 93, 95, 97, 98, 99, 100, 101, 102
Cognitive Career Theory, 24, 93, 97
Cognitive Style, 19, 26, 81, 86, 88, 89, 90
Creed, 19, 21, 25, 28, 76, 96, 101

H

Health Impacts of, 21
Optimism, i, iii, 5, 19, 20, 21, 22, 23, 28, 40, 41, 48, 49, 51, 55, 57, 60, 77, 96, 98, 101, 102
Pessimism, 48, 62

I

Immigration, i, ii, iii, 2, 11, 12, 15, 27, 41, 50, 51, 67, 69, 91, 94, 95, 98, 101, 107
Income, 16, 43, 66, 103, 104

118   *Index*

J

Job Search, 11, 22, 63, 109

L

Lazarus, 20, 98
Lent, Brown & Hackett, 24, 25, 85, 97, 99, 100

O

Optimism, i, iii, 1, 5, 6, 7, 9, 19, 20, 21, 23, 28, 32, 33, 38, 40, 41, 48, 49, 51, 55, 57, 60, 75, 76, 77, 82, 83, 84, 85, 89, 90, 91, 96, 98, 101, 102
    And Barriers, 9, 10, 19, 25, 40, 49, 55, 76, 78, 81
    And Challenges, 1, 7, 27, 77, 86, 91
    And Control, 68, 82, 83, 88, 90, 91
    And Flexibility, 81
    And Satisfaction, 91

P

Pessimism, 20, 22, 41, 48, 62, 75, 80, 83
    And Chance, 54, 68, 69, 83
    And Control, 68, 82, 83, 88, 90, 91
    And Opportunity, 112
Positive Psychology, 5, 20, 75, 77, 82, 90

Psychological Stress, 15

R

Resilience, 23, 24, 77, 93, 97, 99, 101
Retraining Experience, 5, 7, 18, 19, 24, 33, 36, 37, 38, 41, 50, 54, 55, 57, 58, 62, 64, 71, 76, 79, 80, 84, 90, 91, 110, 111, 112, 113

S

Self-Efficacy, i, iii, 1, 5, 6, 7, 9, 19, 24, 25, 26, 27, 28, 32, 33, 38, 40, 41, 69, 70, 72, 74, 75, 76, 84, 85, 87, 88, 89, 90, 91, 94, 96, 97, 98, 99, 100, 102, 111
Self-Esteem, 21, 25, 38, 59, 62, 63, 73, 76, 108
Seligman, 5, 20, 49, 61, 75, 82, 89, 102
Skilled Worker Category, 10
Social Cognitive Theory, 24, 99
Subjective Insight, 18

T

Transitional Difficulties, 9, 10
    Individualism, 12
    Language Barriers, 10, 11, 49, 94
    Survival jobs, 13, 14, 15, 42, 44, 47, 48